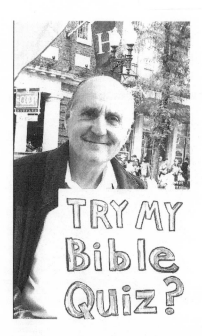

Who is the Harvard Square Bible Guy?

Bruce Benson is a Christian. He's never darkened the door of a Bible school — God blessed him with good books and teachers. He's not ordained by a denomination, so nobody's telling him what to say — and he's not trying to recruit anybody.

Bruce loves to talk about the Bible. He went to Harvard Square and silently held a sign which led to conversations and a surprise: Bruce was thrilled to discover that when he shared truths from the Bible, he'd see faces light up. They understood — they got aha moments.

In *AHA moments from the Bible,* Bruce is bringing Harvard Square to you, drawn from his thousands of spontaneous encounters over seven years.

Christ, the outdoor preacher.
The two greatest things ever written, the Ten Commandments
and the Sermon on the Mount, were delivered in the open air.
It was an open air religion that Jesus founded.

- author unknown

Bruce sets up his outdoor ministry under an umbrella in Harvard Square, summer 2016

AHA
moments
from the
Bible

Answers to the hard questions people on the street are asking

Bruce Benson
The Harvard Square Bible Guy

Heart Wish Books
When knowing God becomes your delight,
then God will give you the wishes of your heart.
Psalm 37:4

AHA moments from the Bible:
Answers to the hard questions people on the street are asking

Published by Heart Wish Books
www.heartwishbooks.com
editor@heartwishbooks.com

Designed by Vera Benson
Photographs on back cover, pages 1, 2, 124, 170 & 196: Apple Benson
Used by permission

All Scripture quotations are the author's paraphrase unless marked

Scripture quotations marked (KJV) are from the King James Version in the public domain

Scripture quotation marked (CEV) is from the Contemporary English Version Copyright © 1991, 1992, 1995 by American Bible Society, used by permission

Scripture quotation marked (NIV) is taken from the Holy Bible, New International Version ®, NIV ®. Copyright © 1973, 1978, 1984, 2011 by Biblica, Inc.™ Used by permission of Zondervan. All rights reserved worldwide. www.zondervan.com The "NIV" and "New International Version" are trademarks registered in the United States Patent and Trademark Office by Biblica, Inc.™

Library of Congress Control Number: 2018905138   ISBN: 978-0999803950
Religion - Christianity - Apologetics

Contents

Chapter One   The Brazil Nut Factor

Chapter Two   Conversations

Chapter Three   Things people ask about God

Chapter Six   The Holy Spirit

Chapter Seven   Being a Christian

Chapter Eight What did Jesus mean?

Chapter Nine Life and death

Chapter Ten   Money

Chapter Eleven   It's not what you've been told

Chapter Twelve Beyond the Brazil Nut Factor

This book is especially for you, in every place on earth
the ones the world calls losers, calls uneducated, foolish, and unworthy
for the poor in spirit, the people who are in pain and suffering
who hunger and thirst for what is right
so you will learn that God loves you

and for Apple Benson, surprise daughter of my old age
your friendship means more to me than you could know

Recently while reading my friend Stuart Diamond's website *Humane Evangelism*, I found the following "street account" about the beginnings of my Bible Quiz in Harvard Square. It will help you see me from an observer's point of view.

Every Christian has their own unique walk with Christ. Stuart has a degree from a Bible college, but he felt his calling was to preach on the street, which he's been doing for decades.

An early version of the Harvard Square Bible Quiz

Foreword from an observer

The following is the most important street account I've ever written. It proves what extraordinary things God can do through an ordinary person. Proves – *"My grace is sufficient for you, for My power is made perfect in weakness."*

I want to show you what God is doing through this person, Bruce Benson. If you knew him like I do and for as long as I have, you wouldn't believe what is happening.

Bruce is average looking. Like the milk you pick up at the market. So ordinary, so average, you never even think about the container or its content. For decades he has waged a daily battle with OCD. He has unnatural fears when out among society. They plague his being. There is a history of severe mental illness in his family.

Bruce studies the Bible like no one I've known in thirty-one years of being a Christian. Four to five hours every single day. It literally keeps him sane. Last fall he'd meet me at Downtown Crossing with "the Quiz." On plain lined paper Bruce had begun constructing a Bible quiz. The outgrowth of his love for the Word of God and thirst to know it.

All the questions were handwritten in ink. Wonderful questions. I would get him to follow me around and ask me some of his questions. A great learning experience for me.

Bruce told me of other Christians who got offended at his Quiz. They were clearly suspicious of his motives — sometimes rebuking him and portraying what he was doing in a bad light. Curious, because there is not a hint of pride in Bruce. He is flat out humble.

Fall came and went. Winter arrived. I disappeared from Boston. Spring sprung. Bruce went down to Harvard Square in Cambridge with one of those silver wire carts that old folk use to bring their groceries home from the supermarket. Laid a board across the top and stacked his Biblical reference material on it. Concordances, lexicons, Hebrew-Greek study material etc., with a hand lettered sign above reading:

Learn how to study the Bible and think for yourself

And Bruce stands there with a sign in hand:

Try my Bible Quiz? Free!

Attached to the front of the shopping cart is an off-white shoe storage hanger. In each of the fifteen or so pouches are handwritten tracts Bruce has composed and photocopied. All original and intellectually thought provoking. All standing on solid biblical ground.

This is meeting with wild success. All manner of persons are stopping to take the Quiz. Folk from Harvard U., lots of Jews, Christians and not, sundry citizens. Last time I observed, Bruce would ask what degree of difficulty of questioning each individual wanted. It is like an avalanche. Gaining momentum. It is one of the few things people are doing in the name of Christ which I believe, with zero doubt, was initiated by God and is being sustained by God.

And, so very happily, it has transformed Bruce's existence. Formerly hermit-like, now he is totally integrated with humankind and driven with a sense of purpose. Best of all, Bruce is amassing a dauntingly deep comprehension of Scripture that all of us should envy.

Stuart Diamond
Humane Evangelism
Spring 2010

Hello from Bruce

I'm in love with the Bible. I love digging into it, going back and forth through its pages, and thinking about its truths. The greatest pleasure I've ever experienced is getting to know God by studying the Bible, and then sharing that knowledge with others.

In this book I want to explain profound truths from the Bible in simple words that are easy to read and easy to understand. This isn't a polished, academic book. It tells the story of a homemade ministry, and real comments made by people on the street. This book is a little rough around the edges, like its author.

Do you think I'm disqualified from writing a book about the Bible because of my past sins? Or my current sins? Or because I don't have a degree or church ordination? Then you'd be making the assumption that *anyone* is qualified or that it's the *person* who makes themselves qualified. No, it's God who chooses, and ordains, and teaches, and calls. Because He is God, He can ordain anyone He wants. So my qualifications don't come from anyone except God.

Do you think God said to Himself, *"I've got to search all over the world to find a perfect person,"* and then He found me? No, God said, let Me find a foolish thing — an unsophisticated person. First Corinthians 1:27 says God chooses the foolish people of the world in order to shame those who think they are wise.

God can do anything. God created everything in our universe. He can take someone the world sees as foolish and use them to teach the Bible, bring the gospel, and offer salvation to people. God does that to find out who's sincere. A person who is proud will reject the truth if it comes from someone who is unsophisticated, but a sincere person is willing to hear the truth from anyone.

Why does God choose the foolish? It's to teach us that He's the one doing it — that it's by His power. He can choose an obedient foolish person and give them understanding, wisdom, and abilities. That's why you're holding this book written by me — a foolish thing of the world. I want to tell all of you who are the same as me, that *you are worthy*. You can study the Bible and ask God for wisdom. James 1:5-6 says God will give you wisdom when you ask in faith.

You can interpret and teach the Bible whether you're male, female, a child, elderly, a professional person, or laborer; whether you're a university professor or mentally handicapped. You don't need permission or approval from a Bible school or a church. It's between you and God. And God loves you.

The questions and answers in this book explain the Bible in a way that's meant to get you started and direct you to the Bible. They are meant to demystify the Bible, make it feel less daunting, make you realize that you *can* understand the Bible — anyone can. I want to get you interested. You get one trip through a very brief life here on earth. *What will you do with the life God gave you? What do you want to contribute to this world? What do you want to be known for?* Now is the time to seek God in the Bible. Be known for that. A wise person doesn't wait until their life is threatened to call out to God.

I'm not asking you for anything. I'm not asking you to join my church, give me a donation, become a monthly partner, pay me tithes, put yourself under authority to me, be baptized into my church, or to just listen to me and not listen to anyone else. I'm not asking you to do anything, say anything, pray anything, or promise anything.

I'm saying: Here! Here's what you need — God's Word, the Bible. Now go — you're free. Go to God and see where He leads you.

Chapter One

The Brazil Nut Factor

Dear Lord God,
When I found Your Word, the Holy Bible,
I felt like a person who finds a treasure chest full of money:
— overflowing with happy excitement.

— Psalm 119:162

The Brazil Nut Factor is a person.

God puts them in your path to present the Bible to you in a way that clicks, and you see God in a new light.

That's your first aha moment.

Now you see the Bible as interesting and attractive, and you want to hear more.

Meet my Brazil Nut Factor

On a summer day in 1983, I was walking through the downtown area of Providence, Rhode Island, when I saw a man standing on a corner. He was a street preacher talking about the Bible. I just caught the last few minutes of his talk, but there was one thing he said that pleased my mind:

"If I need a vitamin that's in Brazil nuts,
then God's gonna make sure I eat some Brazil nuts."

Wow, now that's interesting, that's appealing. I'd heard preachers before, but I never heard that. It got me. It made God feel real to me — that He cares about me, thinks about me, understands me. It brought God down to earth. That was my first aha moment.

God moved the preacher just for me

And the preacher said one other thing — he talks every weekday at lunchtime. I was determined to go back. I wanted to hear more. So the next day, I went back to the same spot at twelve noon with some Brazil nuts. But he wasn't there. What? Where is he? So I wandered down the street. Fortunately, I went in the right direction, because I found him two blocks from where he had been the previous day.

I listened to his hour-long talk, and when he was done I approached him. He looked at me and said, "What are you, a Buddhist?"
I said, "No, I'm like you."
And then I said, "I got you some Brazil nuts."
He said, "I like cashews."
So I said, "Let's go get some cashews."
There actually was a nut store nearby. So we went and got some cashews. He told me his name: Tilman Gandy. And we became friends.

After I met Tilman, I stayed in Providence for seven years. Every day for that seven years, Tilman always had a regular spot where he preached. It was the spot where I found him on the second day, when I brought the Brazil nuts. He never moved from that spot. It wasn't until years later that it hit me what happened the day I saw Tilman for the first time.

I had a habit of walking the same route through downtown every day, which I stubbornly stuck to. The regular spot where Tilman preached was not on that route. I was stunned when I realized what God had done. God had to move Tilman for *one day* to a corner that was on my route, so I would see him and hear what he said about the Brazil nuts. I never did ask Tilman why he moved on that one day to the spot where I saw him the first time.

God is amazing — He can do anything. And thank God for Brazil nuts.

My teacher Tilman

I moved into the rooming house where Tilman lived. God used that man to till my hard head and plant the seed of the Word of God. Tilman impressed upon me the importance of the Bible. He gave me a good start — a solid foundation. Right away I could see that Tilman had understanding, and I wanted to hear every word he said.

Tilman turned out to be one of the most unusual, interesting people I've ever met. He'd never set foot in a Bible school, never wrote a book, never taught in a school — but he was really special.

I was a baby Christian — I knew nothing. But with my street preacher friend Tilman, I was like a child being taught their ABCs by an old university professor. Most people who saw Tilman preach ignored him; some mocked and scoffed. But God gave me eyes to see that he had the best thing — it was gold. He had the Bible, God's Word. I was smart enough to know what I'd found, and I just listened. God had led me to a hidden gem. That was my encounter with the Brazil Nut Factor.

 Once when I was listening to Tilman teach, I realized that the Old Testament *foreshadowed* things that would happen in the New Testament hundreds and even thousands of years later. It made me think, "Wow, the Bible is true."

As I studied the Bible on my own, I found myself creating questions that would teach a lesson, not knowing that I would eventually use those questions for my own street ministry.

THE BRAZIL NUT FACTOR
It was like God made a Bible teacher just for me, who would say just the thing that would make the Bible and Christianity attractive to me. My hope is that my ministry will have that same effect on someone.

I'm trying to make the Bible come alive for you

There's not a perfect Bible teacher on the planet
Every pastor, scholar, or church denomination is getting *something* wrong. Look around. One pastor says this, another pastor says that. If two say exactly the opposite, obviously they can't both be right.

No doubt people are going to disagree with things I've said
They may not like my paraphrases of Bible passages. I could have labored over this book for ten more years. I could have brought in a team of Bible scholars. Guess what: it still wouldn't be perfect. But I've put in this book what I've learned over the years, and where my studies have led me after conversations on the street with thousands of people.

I got into the Bible because of a street preacher
You've never seen a street preacher like Tilman Gandy. He would say things like, "Noah was on the ark eating hot dogs and potato chips and drinking iced tea." Now that's not perfect because the Bible doesn't say Noah ate hot dogs. The original Hebrew text of the Old Testament doesn't say that Noah ate potato chips. Scholars could debate whether or not Noah drank iced tea. But that street preacher made Noah's ark come alive. It made me listen — it made Noah's ark real to me. That's what I mean when I say I'm trying to make the Bible come alive for you.

If you're interested in how I went from being a baby Christian to becoming a street preacher and then writing a book about the Bible (or want to try my Bible Quiz), you'll find that in Chapter Twelve: "Beyond the Brazil Nut Factor."

Chapter Two

Conversations

A Christian comes to you as a go-between, an agent.
Christ is speaking to you, calling you through the Christian,
urging you to do your part to make peace with God.

- 2 Corinthians 5:20

Many of the questions and answers in *AHA moments from the Bible* are drawn directly from my conversations with strangers on the street who came up to me because of my sign offering a Bible Quiz. As it turned out, *they* would often quiz *me*.

Some of the best material came from encounters with the most angry people. Their accusations against God gave me incentives to dig into the Bible to prove that God's ways are always right.

Each topic has Scripture references you can use as a way to study God's Word. Just open to any page and be fed Bible bites that you can think about as you walk down the street, sit at your table, or lie on your bed (Deuteronomy 6:5-7).

Enjoying a friendly conversation in Newport, Rhode Island, 2012

Street preachers have conversations?

Do you think a street preacher is a bitter person who won't listen to you — who just talks at you in a condescending tone, yells in your face, calls you a heathen, and seems to look forward to watching you burn in hell?

I am a different kind of street preacher. And there is support in the Bible for what I do. Acts 17:2 says the apostle Paul went to the people and reasoned with them from the Bible. Acts 20:2 says Paul preached to the disciples. "Reasoned" and "preached" are both translated from the Greek word *dialegomai*. It sounds like the English word dialogue because that's what it means — to have a conversation.

Like the apostle, I also reason from the Bible. My "preaching" is a back and forth — one person speaks and then listens to the other. This makes for calm, intelligent discussions.

Why the Bible?

The Bible is like any other book in that it has words, pages, and sentences. But what makes the Bible different is its author is God. Therefore the Bible has power in it that no other book has.

That's what makes a question from the Bible so special. When the answer hits you and gives you an aha moment, it makes you believe God — you realize that what He says in the Bible is true. When the Bible works on your mind in that way, it produces faith in your heart. And it's through faith that we receive God's saving grace.

God exists. In the Bible, that's a given. God doesn't start out by introducing Himself and trying to prove to you that He exists. He just starts the Bible by saying, "In the beginning God created ..." You believe or you don't, and if you believe then you study the Bible and come to know God, and learn that He does *in fact* exist.

The purpose of the Bible is to inform us that we are sinners
We choose to rebel against God. We make ourselves His enemies and become hostile to Him because we want to do things our own way. By willfully breaking God's laws we become alienated from Him, wreak havoc, and lead others astray. God says that because of this we deserve death. We can't save ourselves. We have no hope on our own.

The Bible tells us of God's great love for us
It's the story of Jesus Christ, who is God our Savior. God provided the way to restore our relationship with Him — that's what it means to be saved. It's in the Bible that God teaches us the way.

Why is the Bible so big and hard to understand?
That's actually a blessing, because we can spend a lifetime studying the Bible, working through it, in order to get to know God. It occupies our mind and in the process we become more like God, more cleansed of sin — more Christlike. And Hebrews chapter 11 tells us that by studying the Bible — hearing God's Word — we can find our calling: the work that God wants us to do for Him.

Why questions?

JESUS USED QUESTIONS TO GIVE PEOPLE AHA MOMENTS

Jesus asked questions. When Jesus asked a question it wasn't because He didn't know the answer. Jesus used questions as a way to teach, to save souls, to scold, to warn, and to make people face up to a certain sin. Jesus used surgeon-like precision, expertly asking questions in order to seize a person's full attention, jolt their mind, and grab their heart. Making a point by asking questions was a more effective way to convince people than if Jesus had simply made the point in the form of a statement. Jesus used questions to give people aha moments — we know this from their reactions.

The Bible only mentions one thing Jesus did during His childhood. It's in Luke 2:46-49. Jesus was twelve years old. Joseph and His mother found Him in the temple, sitting in the midst of the Bible teachers, questioning them and answering their questions. The first time in the Bible that we are told about Jesus speaking with someone, it was a question and answer session. And we are told that everyone was astonished at the things Jesus spoke.

Why did I decide to use questions?
Thank God that I did. He must have put the idea in my mind. Call it intuition if you like. I saw it as a way to make the Bible enjoyable for people. And when I started doing the Quiz, I realized that through questions I could tell people things in a way that was easier for them to take in, and I was less likely to come across as preachy.

People thought they were just taking a Bible quiz, but they were also feeling the power of God's Word — they were learning wonderful truths from the Bible. They could learn what the gospel is, become aware of their sinfulness and need for the Savior Jesus Christ, and get an understanding of the great love, compassion, and mercy that God feels for them.

During His ministry, Jesus asked hundreds of questions. It was His favorite, most effective way to get through to a person. You can study some of those questions and the reactions of the people Jesus directed them to in the following passages:

- Matthew 21:23-27
- Matthew 22:41-46
- Luke 14:1-6
- John 9:35
- John 18:4,7
- John 21:15-17

"Isn't this the reason you are wrong —
because you do not know the Scriptures or the power of God?"

- **Jesus**, Mark 12:24

Giving out aha moments

I always knew when a sudden realization hit someone. The way their face changed, the sparkle in their eyes — the proverbial light bulb appearing over their head. It made my heart swell up and my eyes wet. I was so grateful that God was letting me share His Word.

When it first started happening I realized the power God had granted me. Groups of young people would come up. I wasn't giving out sex-drugs-and-rock-and-roll. I only gave out one thing — lessons from the Bible. And it amazed me to see young people getting so much pleasure from the Bible.

I couldn't wait to get on the street each day and see who God would send for me to talk to. And at the end of the day I'd go home ecstatic, bubbling with joy, walking on air. I felt I was the most fortunate of men. Now I understood why comedians say they get the greatest pleasure when they make people laugh. I was getting the greatest pleasure using the Bible to give people aha moments.

Best question:
Why is Jesus called a lamb?

This question led to the best aha moments.

First, I'd ask: "Who in the Bible is called the Lamb of God?"
People would say, "That's easy — it's Jesus."
Then I'd say, "Okay, tell me this: a lamb is a baby sheep —
it's an animal. So why would *Jesus* be called a lamb?"

When I gave the answer, I'd see people gasp.

So, why *is* Jesus called a lamb?
Well, are you familiar with Passover? It's one of the most important
events in Israel's history. You can read about Passover in Exodus,
chapter 12. The children of Israel were being held as slaves in Egypt,
and cried out to God for help.

God heard their cry and sent His servant Moses to lead them out of
Egypt. There was a problem though. Egypt's ruler — Pharaoh —
didn't want to let them go. The Egyptians worshipped idols. God
used Pharaoh's stubbornness as an opportunity to show the Egyptians
that He is the one true God — the living God. He sent ten plagues
on the Egyptians. When each of the first nine plagues struck, Pharaoh
said he would let Israel go, but changed his mind as soon as God
removed the plague.

The tenth plague threatened to bring death to the firstborn of every
family in Egypt if Pharaoh didn't let the Israelites go. But God told
Israel there was something they could do so that *their* firstborn
wouldn't die. God told them to get a young lamb. It had to be free
of spots and blemishes. They were to have the lamb live with them
for several days. Then they had to kill the lamb.

They were to take the lamb's blood and put it on their door. Death would *pass over* any house that had the blood of the lamb on its door. That's why it's called Passover.

The children of Israel obeyed God and their firstborn were spared because of the lamb's blood (Exodus 12:13). But not so for the Egyptians — all of their firstborn died. It worked. Pharaoh and all the Egyptians told Israel to go. The Egyptians even gave them silver, gold, clothing, and other necessities to take with them. God delivered His people (Exodus 12:29-42).

God told Israel to remember Passover. Each family was to kill a lamb every year (Exodus 12:14-20). They were to always celebrate how God delivered His people from slavery in Egypt. Also God commanded Israel to sacrifice animals daily in the temple, over and over, as an atonement to God for sin (Leviticus 5:1-19). Taking the life of animals — shedding their blood — was a ritual which was meant to show God's people the seriousness with which God views sin. Animal blood was a temporary covering for sin.

Jesus Christ, the Lamb of God
About 1,500 years after the first Passover in Egypt, John the Baptist saw Jesus walking toward him and said: "Look, it's the Lamb of God who takes away the sin of the world " (John 1:29).

At the end of His ministry, Jesus shed His blood on a cross in Jerusalem on the same day as the yearly Passover observance. As He died, the curtain of the temple was torn from top to bottom, symbolizing that temple rituals were no longer necessary. The blood of Jesus removed the barriers between God and humanity, as it was a sufficient atonement for sin (Matthew 27:51).

The New Testament says that for Christians, Jesus is our Passover Lamb. In 1 Corinthians 5:7, the apostle Paul wrote:

Christ, our Passover, was sacrificed for us.

Christians don't put the blood of our Lamb, Jesus, on our door, but we put His blood on ourselves — so to speak — and *death passes over us*. It means our soul will not die, and we will live with Jesus in heaven — forever.

The sacrifice of Jesus was different because it only needed to be done once, not constantly like the animal sacrifices of the Old Testament. The New Testament uses the word "once" to describe the sacrifice of Jesus:

> When He died, He died once to break the power of sin.
>
> - Romans 6:10

Jesus does not need to be sacrificed every day.

> God's will was for us to be made holy by the sacrifice of the body of Jesus Christ, once for all time.   - Hebrews 10:10

"Once" is translated from the Greek word *ephapax*. It means once, not several times; one time, only once — once for all. The sacrifice of Jesus was permanent, voluntary, and did not just cover sin but removed it (Hebrews 10:1-4, 7-10).

One of the ways God teaches us is by showing us things in the Old Testament that are symbols of what's coming in the New. The lamb that the children of Israel killed at Passover was a symbol. It pointed to God's Lamb, Jesus, who was sinless (free of blemishes) and would give His body as a sacrifice — shed His blood to pay the death penalty for sin because He loves us (John 3:16; Romans 6:23; 1 Peter 1:18-19; 2:21-24)).

When the Lord saw the blood of the lamb on the doors of the Israelites in Egypt, death passed over them. For Christians, God's wrath and condemnation pass over us because of the blood of Christ, God's Lamb. We are delivered from the fear of death.
(Romans 8:1; Ephesians 1:7; Hebrews 2:14-15)

The blood of the Passover lamb in Exodus was shed so that God's people, the Israelites, would be freed from slavery to the Egyptians. The blood of the Lamb of God, Jesus Christ, delivers God's people from slavery to sin. God's people are all those who believe in Jesus Christ as their Lord and Savior (Romans 1:16; 6:18; Galatians 3:26-29).

That's why Jesus is called a lamb, the Lamb of God.
(Isaiah 53:7; Acts 8:32; 1 Peter 1:9; Revelation 5:6-14)

Jesus rose from the dead and lives forever. Anyone who wants to can trust in His sacrifice, be reconciled with God, and live with Him forever (Revelation 1:17-18).

That's what we call the good news — the gospel.

Chapter Three

Things people ask about God

This is what the LORD says …
Those who wish to boast
should boast in this alone:
that they truly know Me
and understand that I am the LORD.

- Jeremiah 9:23-24

When it comes to our feelings toward God, we humans have a bad habit. Occasionally we give God thanks, but what we mostly send His way are accusations, blame, and rejection. God wants us to make the effort to get to know Him, and if we do that, then He will give us the ability to love Him, thank Him, and obey Him.

Why does God allow evil?

I heard "Why does God allow evil?" more than any other question, and it's the most frequent accusation made against God.

The thinking of some people goes like this: "If God allows evil, then why shouldn't I do what I want?"

Why does God allow a five-year-old girl to be gang raped? You're thinking: God knows everything and He can do anything. If *I'm* God and I see the rapists, and I know what they're about to do — I would take one of my lightning bolts and throw it at those rapists and kill them. So why doesn't God do that?

There's a serious problem with that line of reasoning: you're saying *you* can do a better job at being God than God can. You're saying *you* are more compassionate, *you* are more righteous than God.

You're accusing God, and what you're really saying is that God is evil. So we have to ask: "Is God good or is God evil?" The Bible tells us that everything God does is perfectly just and fair, and that He does no wrong (Deuteronomy 32:4).

A man named Job accused God
In the first chapter of the Book of Job, we're told that Job was a good man; he was blameless, a man of complete integrity, one who feared God and stayed away from evil.

Job was the richest person for miles around, and he had seven sons and three daughters who lived a good life. But all of a sudden, Job was hit with one catastrophe after another. All of his animals were either stolen or killed, his servants were killed, his ten children were killed, and he was struck with a painful illness.

Job didn't know the reason why all these things were happening to him. Job had three friends who convinced him that God was causing the catastrophes. They said, "Job, confess, what evil thing did you do to cause God to strike you this way?"

Job said, "That's not fair, I've done nothing wrong to deserve this." So Job began making all sorts of accusations against God. Job charged God with being unjust, and he wanted answers from God (Job 27:2; 31:35).

Job wanted God put on trial

God granted Job's wish. But beginning in chapter 38, God turned the tables and questioned Job, asking him to explain things like where light comes from, and how the oceans are contained. God asked Job, "Did you give the horse his strength? Did you give the peacock her wings?" (Job 39:13,19).

Job couldn't answer God's questions. Job couldn't explain how God created everything or how nature works. God showed Job that he wasn't qualified to judge God.

God is Almighty.
He has His reasons for doing what He does.
Job realized his error and said to God,
"I take back everything I said, and sit in dust and ashes to show my repentance" (Job 42:1-6).

We had nothing to do with creating anything: not our bodies, the air we breathe — or our very life. How can we chastise God? *How dare we sit in judgment against the One who gives us life?*

So, back to the question, "Why does God let innocent, defenseless children be raped, tortured, and murdered?" The answer is found in the Book of Job — it's the wrong question!

If that's the wrong question, then what's the *right* question?
The right question is this: "God, will you forgive me, a sinner?"
(Micah 6:8; Luke 18:10-14; James 4:6).

Did God create evil?

The King James Version (KJV) translation of Isaiah 45:7 has God saying: "I form the light, and create darkness: I make peace, and create evil: I the Lord do all these things."

In 1611 when the KJV was translated, people knew what was meant by "evil" in this verse. It does not mean the evil of sin. God did not create the evil of sin, God does not sin, and He never tempts anyone to sin (James 1:12-16). What the KJV meant by "evil" was calamity, disaster, bad times, discord, trouble, adversity ... that's what God creates for His own purposes

It's not evil when God creates calamity. He can choose to send calamity to punish the wicked and protect the innocent (Isaiah 47:9-11). And He can allow calamity to test, strengthen, and mature His faithful followers (Hebrews 12:5-11). Everything God does is good (Deuteronomy 32:4).

 ## *We* create evil when we sin

We sin when we disobey God's laws in the Bible (1 John 3:4). God gave us the freedom to choose to disobey. When we love God, we choose to obey Him. God won't force anyone to obey Him.

The first one who chose to create evil by disobeying God was Lucifer:

> Look at yourself Lucifer ...
> You weren't content to be one of My brightest stars.
> You wanted to climb the ranks.
> You thought you could be Me, take my place, sit on My throne.
> And as a result you have fallen — all the way down to the pit.
>
> - Isaiah 14:12-15

Why does the Bible say God is jealous?

When a famous television personality heard the preacher in her church say, "The Lord our God is a jealous God," she commented, "Something about that didn't feel right in my spirit." She wondered, if God is so great, why would He be jealous of her?

In the Ten Commandments, in Exodus 20:2-5, God said:

> I am the Lord your God …
> Do not worship or serve any other gods
> because I, the Lord your God, am a jealous God.

God is our Creator. He is our King — our Lord. He has every right to demand our respect and that we worship Him and no other.

 God is not jealous *of* us, He is jealous *for* us

When the Bible says God is jealous, it really means He is "zealous" for those He loves, and doesn't want them worshipping false gods who can't save them. God wants people to be faithful to Him so He can give them eternal life.

God's jealousy is without sin. God's jealousy comes from wanting what's best for us. God's jealousy is holy, just like His anger and love. God alone is our Savior. Only He gives life. Worshipping any person or thing other than God will only bring us eternal death. That's why God is jealous for us — He wants us to live and not die.

(Isaiah 43:11; 2 Corinthians 11:1-3)

Is God a sadist?

The Bible teaches that many people will not be allowed to spend eternity with God in heaven. But God's justice does *not* require Him to burn them in flames forever. This portrayal has given the world a false idea of who God is.

What if a church near you offers a free lecture to explain what they believe. So you go, and hear this:

> *"Welcome everyone to the Last Church in Boston.*
> *We want to tell you how you can live forever in heaven, while*
> *listening to the screams of your loved ones who didn't make it,*
> *as God fries them like strips of bacon for all eternity."*

I bet you wouldn't join them if they *were* the last church in Boston. I'm not saying there's no such place as hell. There is. But hell is kind of like God saying, "I don't want *you* in *My* house."

The Bible is filled with figures of speech. And then there's everything that's not figures of speech. In order to correctly interpret the Bible, we have to know which is which. It makes all the difference.

And in order to be able to know the difference, we need to study the Bible diligently and, more importantly, we need to pray for God-given common sense. My diligent Bible study and God-given common sense tells me that God will NOT be frying screaming people like strips of bacon.

So what will He do with the ones He doesn't want in His house?
He will extinguish them — blot them out. They will be no more, and it will be as though they never existed. On the next page, I've provided a few Bible passages to start you off on your own study.

In 2 Thessalonians 1:9 we're told that those who go to hell will be punished with <u>everlasting destruction</u>. But in Matthew 10:28, Jesus said, "Don't fear those who kill the body, and are not able to kill the soul: but rather fear Him who is able to <u>destroy</u> both soul and body in hell." The word "destroy" means to kill or abolish, and this is called the *second death* (Revelation 2:11).

> First we read that those in hell will be punished with everlasting destruction, and then we're told that God will kill their souls in hell. Is it a contradiction? No, there are no contradictions in the Bible. "Everlasting destruction" is poetic — a figure of speech; "kill the soul" is literal — not a figure of speech.

Revelation 14:11 says those in hell have no rest day or night, and the smoke of their torment rises up <u>forever and ever</u>. But in John 3:16, Jesus said God loves the world so much that He sent His only Son, Jesus, to die on a cross, so that whoever chooses to believe in Him, will not <u>perish</u>, but have <u>everlasting life</u>. The word "perish" means permanent absolute destruction.

> The smoke rising "forever and ever" is poetic, but "perish" is actual fact — literal. By comparing Bible verse with Bible verse, I conclude that *everlasting destruction* means irreversible death (finis, no mas). But *everlasting life* means just that — living forever with Jesus, the Savior.

In Jude 1:7 we read that Sodom and Gomorrah are presented as an example, suffering the punishment of eternal fire. Is Sodom still burning? Of course not — they were consumed.

 Hebrews 12:29 says: "Our God is an utterly consuming fire." *The souls of those who choose hell will be consumed spiritually and cease to exist* (Psalm 37:20). God won't torture them. Our God is not a sadist.

Is God guilty of genocide?

Some people want God to be put on trial for genocide.

What did God do?
God ordered the Israelites to kill everyone in Canaan except for Rahab and her family (Deuteronomy 20:16-17).

God's accusers say He did that because He's racist, He's a murderer, He's unforgiving. First of all, what God did to Canaan is none of our business — it's between God and the people of Canaan. But let's look at the accusations anyway (John 21:21-22).

Is God racist?
No, God doesn't kill people because of their race. He killed the Canaanites because they engaged in the most perverted sexual and religious practices — they even burned their children alive as sacrifices to their god Molech (Leviticus 18:1-30; Acts 10:34-35).

Is God a murderer?
When God kills, it's not murder. God created us — we have no life apart from Him (John 1:3; 15:4-5). God is our King, Lawgiver, Judge, Jury and Executioner (Isaiah 33:22; Revelation 20:15). He has the right and obligation to do with us as He sees fit (Job 40:1-2, 6-9; Romans 11:33-36).

Is God unforgiving?
No. God waited four hundred years before destroying the Canaanites. God gave them time to repent — He wanted to forgive them. God waited until their wickedness reached the point of no return before He told Israel to kill them all (Genesis 15:16; 1 Timothy 2:4; 2 Peter 3:9).

The Canaanites knew what they were doing was wrong. They heard about God and His might, but refused to turn from their evil and follow Him (Romans 1:18-20). Rahab was a Canaanite. She heard about

God, gave her heart to Him, and God forgave her and spared her (Joshua 2:1-21; Psalm 11:4-7).

God is Love, Holiness, and Justice. Because God is Love, He must also be Justice. God doesn't take pleasure in the death of the wicked (Ezekiel 33:11). God is patient and merciful, but He must eventually execute justice, or He would also be wicked (Proverbs 24:24; 1 John 4:8,16).

God is holy, and God calls His people to be holy. Israel therefore had to be holy. God gave Israel His laws so they could teach them to the other nations. And through Israel would come Jesus Christ who would offer salvation to all nations (Isaiah 42:6; 1 Peter 1:15-16).

God wanted to wipe out the Canaanites so Israel wouldn't be influenced by them. And God was right. Israel failed to kill all the Canaanites who continued to live among them. Many Israelites were influenced to take up the Canaanites' evil religious and sexual practices (Deuteronomy 7:1-16; Judges 1:27-36; 1 Kings 14:22-24).

When God told Israel to kill all the Canaanites, He was teaching Israel that sin is serious. God made an example out of Canaan. He wants us to learn from their misdeeds and change our ways, because one day God will judge the world for the last time (Deuteronomy 13:10-11; Romans 6:23; 11:22; 1 Corinthians 10:11; Revelation 20:11-15).

 Thank God that He killed the Canaanites. It shows how much He loves us. God is not a genocidal maniac. *He's a loving Father who wants to protect His children like any father would.* The devil would like you to worship Molech and go to hell.

Yes, God's anger and punishment are severe. But Jesus Christ, God with us, let Himself be tortured to death to save us from the ultimate punishment: death of the soul. God is compassionate, kind, and gracious. He hears the cries of all who sincerely seek Him (Psalm 34:15, 17-19; 86:15; John 3:16; Hebrews 2:14).

Isn't God anti-war?

There are Christian pastors and others in important places who say things like "war isn't Christian" and "Jesus is against war because Jesus is the Prince of Peace, and Jesus taught only peace" (Isaiah 9:6). Are they right?

Some people march in anti-war protests carrying signs that say:

BEAT YOUR SWORDS INTO PLOWSHARES

They think they are piously citing the Bible, when all they've done is lifted and misused a line from Isaiah 2:4. They obviously don't know that in Joel 3:10, God said:

BEAT YOUR PLOWSHARES INTO SWORDS

How can both be true? The answer is in the Book of Ecclesiastes where God tells us:

> To every thing there is a season and a time to every purpose under the heavens ... a time to kill, and a time to heal ...
> a time to love, and a time to hate; a time of war, and a time of peace.   (see Ecclesiastes 3:1-8)

But wait, doesn't one of the Ten Commandments say, "Thou shall not kill"? No, that's not what God wrote.

What God actually said is,"Thou shall not commit murder" (Exodus 20:13). We know this from God-given common sense, because in the Bible God commands that there be governments, and that governments have armies and police forces. It's the government's job to kill those who attack our nation, and apprehend, contain, and sometimes kill criminals (Genesis 9:5-6; Romans 13:1-5).

The commandment cannot possibly be "Thou shall not kill" because then God would be contradicting Himself, which He does not do. Therefore, the commandment is "Thou shall not commit murder."

Protecting the innocent from those who wish them evil is a very dear thing to God. He saved the nation of Israel by destroying the army of Pharaoh in the Red Sea. And then Moses and the children of Israel sang to God:

> ... the Lord triumphed gloriously ...
> The Lord is a man of war: the Lord is His name.
>
> (see Exodus 15:1-4)

God still hates evil just as much as He always has.

People are not handling the Word of God correctly when they argue that governments should never wage war because Jesus is the Prince of Peace. God tells us in 2 Timothy 2:15 that when Christians study the Bible we are to make a straight cut, and correctly measure off and mark out the portions of Scripture. It means you must never put something where it doesn't belong.

 We have to know when an instruction in the Bible is referring to *personal interactions* with other people, and when it's referring to the duties of the government.

If a Christian feels led to serve their country in the military or law enforcement, that is an honorable and blessed calling. David, king of Israel, wrote:

> *Blessed is the Lord who is my strength —*
> *who trains my hands for war and my fingers for battle.*
>
> - Psalm 144:1

How does God feel about police?

In July of 2016, five police officers were murdered in Dallas, Texas, and other officers were wounded. The next day when I did my Bible Quiz in Harvard Square, I put up a small sign which read, "Pray for the Police." I was shocked at the reaction. It was about ten unfavorable to every one favorable. People yelled in my face, called me names, and expressed their anger and disgust over my sign. I thought to myself, *These are heartless, evil people. Have they no feelings for the officers' families?* What really broke my heart was hearing the same condemnation from fellow Christians. They should know better.

Why do we *have* police?

We have police because God gave them to us. Thank God for that. God gave us governments and the government hires police. We *need* police, because if there were no police then rapists and murderers could run free. We would live in constant fear and lose our freedom. God wants the police to be armed. Why? God wants criminals to fear the police. If a criminal knows they could get shot, they might think twice about raping you. Did I say that law-abiding citizens should be afraid of the police? No, I didn't.

If you want to get along with the police there are two things you need to do: First, don't commit crimes. Secondly, when you interact with the police — comply with their instructions.

Am I getting these things from the Bible?

Yes, in Romans 13:1-5, where the apostle Paul wrote:

Every person must obey the authorities who are in power over them. There is no authority that has not been put in place by God. *They are in authority over you because God gave them that authority.*

Therefore, anyone who chooses to reject the governing authority and stand in defiance against it is really choosing to wage war against God. And if you fight against God you will only bring condemnation upon yourself.

The authorities do not strike fear in the hearts of those who do what's right, but those who do evil. Are you willing to not be afraid of the authorities? Then do the things that are good and right. And if you do, the authorities will show their approval.

The reason those in authority can do these things is because they are working for God. *And God put them there as a force for good — your good.* But if you decide to pursue evil then be afraid — be filled with fear because God has invested His designated authorities with the power of life and death. They are His servants, representing Him, and satisfying His anger by carrying out the work of exacting vengeance upon those who do evil.

So, God is helping us to avoid evil in two ways. First, each of us has a conscience, that God-given, inherent ability to tell right from wrong. And in addition, there's the desire to avoid being punished by His chosen authorities.

- Romans 13:1-5

Why should we pray for the police when some of them are bad?
A fellow Christian saw my pray-for-the-police sign and called me uneducated. He thought it was wrong to pray for the police because of all the evils that black people have been subjected to in America, sometimes even at the hands of the police. Of course I'm not ignorant of those things. I personally feel America owes black people an apology and compensation for the wrongs done to them.

But there's something worse than being uneducated, and that's being biblically illiterate. The apostle Paul wrote a letter to Timothy in which God told us to pray for all those who are in authority in our government. And that includes the police who represent the government and act on its behalf. God told us to make heartfelt prayers for the police — for their good, that they be blessed. We should pray that they are safe and protected. And yes, we are to pray that they do their job according to God's will (1 Timothy 2:1-2).

When Paul wrote that, he was living under the government of the Roman emperor Nero who was fond of torturing Christians. North Korea tortures and murders Christians. But it's been reported that the Christians in North Korea are not praying for the death of the leader of the country, and they're not even praying for regime change. What they're praying for is that the leader of North Korea will come to Christ.

When my fellow Christian called me uneducated, he was calling God uneducated. When God put Romans 13:1-5 and 1 Timothy 2:1-2 in the Bible, do you think God didn't know that black people would be treated in an evil way in America? Do you think God didn't know that some police would be bad apples? Of course God knew those things. Yes, there's some bad police. That's because the only ones God could use to be police are humans. But most police are the salt of the earth. We rarely hear about the selfless acts they do every day. They face down very dangerous people so we can go about our lives in safety. They lay their life on the line for us and even give their life. The Bible calls that the greatest love (John 15:13).

Is it ever okay to disobey the police?

If a police officer ordered you to commit murder you would have to refuse because obeying that order would cause you to disobey God's commandment which forbids murder (Exodus 20:13). But you can't decide to disobey because the officer didn't give you your proper respect or you didn't like his tone. If you decide to disobey a police officer's instructions, you need to be sure you're right. God is watching.

One Bible for black and white

Now maybe you want to say to me, "Bruce, you don't know what you're talking about — you're white. You have no idea what it's like being black." Yes, I'm white, but you know who's not white or black?

God. And God didn't write one Bible for black people and a different Bible for white people. God wrote one Bible. And in that one Bible, God made one set of rules which apply to every person.

Why did my sign say "Pray for the Police"?

Someone asked me why I never had a sign that said, Pray for the Victims of Criminal Police? Okay, they might have a point. Yes, of course, pray for them and be angry. But that's all over the news — people *are* doing that. My job is to expose deception. The anger in Harvard Square over my sign was caused by the deception that the police force as an institution is evil, or that all police are evil. You hear the calls for prayer for the victims of crimes done by police. But in the media and even in churches, you're not being told that God ordained the police, they work for Him, and God wants us to pray for the police too. So I put up my sign. Someone had to say it.

Be careful who you get involved with

You're angry that some white police have mistreated and even murdered black people. And you should be angry. God's angry about it too, and He will get justice. But you want to work for change. Okay; do your homework first. Be aware. There are groups that sound good, who claim to be working for the good of black people — but it's a trap. They're really working to promote hatred of police, and lawlessness. They call police officers "pigs" and say things like "off the pigs," which means "murder the police." They spread the lie that every time a white officer shoots a black person it's because of racism. And then they celebrate when police officers are insulted, physically harmed, or murdered. Do you think it's right to incite violence against all police officers because of the evil done by a few? Remember Romans 13:1-5, the Bible passage we began with: whatever evil you do to the police — God sees it as being done to Him. God will punish you if you support anti-police groups like that (2 Corinthians 6:14-17).

Race hustlers

The truth is, black people and white people mostly get along just fine. Most of us don't judge each other by race or color — we see each other as fellow human beings. Unfortunately, though, there are people who want to divide us. They're called "race hustlers." Some of them pretend to be Christians. Some even tack the word "reverend" or "bishop" in front of their name to fool people into giving them respect and credibility. They use color and race to pit people against the police and against each other, looking for any opportunity to exploit and deceive. Let's say no to the race hustlers. They don't do any good. They cause pain and death. They're just in it for money, power, and their own glory.

How do I deal with the pain of injustice?
Another man came up to me, a middle-aged black man who saw my pray-for-the-police sign and didn't like it. He said he was a Christian and told me about the time when he was young and was sleeping on a beach with some white friends. A white police officer came and woke them up. The police officer woke his white friends gently. But when he got to him, the police officer kicked him in the head.

That Christian black man has been holding a grudge against the white police officer for decades. What he has to do is forgive that police officer and pray that the officer comes to Christ and that Jesus takes his racism from him (Matthew 5:44). Okay, fine. But that's not the solution to racist police who commit crimes against black people, even murder. Right. So you could study law, become an attorney or a politician, or go into law enforcement yourself. You could work on screening and training of police officers, and find ways to reduce the possibility of wrongdoing.

What's the first thing you should do?
So, it's simple. God wants you to comply with police officers, even the racist ones. Don't hold a grudge, don't let it destroy you when you're slighted or worse by police officers. Don't seek revenge and don't feel good when others take revenge on the police. Easy, right? No, it's hard — unless you follow Christ. You can do all those things and more through Christ (Philippians 4:13).

Was God cruel to rape victims?

A teenage girl came up to me at the Quiz and told me all her friends say God is evil and cruel because He forced women who were raped to marry the men who raped them. They get that idea from people who hate God and spread lies about Him and, tragically, also from so-called Christian scholars and Bible translators.

Throw away your Bible if it's a New International Version Bible, the NIV. Why? Because the NIV Bible says this:

> If a man happens to meet a virgin who is not pledged to be married and <u>rapes</u> her and they are discovered, he shall pay her father fifty shekels of silver. He must marry the young woman, for he violated her. He can never divorce her as long as he lives.   - Deuteronomy 22:28-29 (NIV)

That is a lie. God never said that, nor would He ever. Their so-called translation is a vile slander against God. It has caused much damage to the cause of Christ — to the sharing of the gospel of Christ.

You need to know that when men translate the Bible into various versions, they sometimes have a tendency to force their own ideas into the text. Here's another translation of these same verses. This is the Contemporary English Version (CEV):

> Suppose a woman isn't engaged to be married, and a man <u>talks her into sleeping with him</u>. If they are caught, they will be forced to get married. He must give her father fifty pieces of silver as a bride price and can never divorce her.
>   - Deuteronomy 22:28-29 (CEV)

It's very different, right? And it gives the true meaning of the passage.

In these verses we just looked at, God is talking about a young woman who sneaks off with a male friend and engages in sexual intercourse. It is not about rape. It's about an unmarried man and woman who both willingly engage in premarital sex. God is saying — *that* is only for marriage. So if you do it, you *are* married. You will follow the rules, get legally married, and stay married for life.

Why would God give such a law against sex outside of marriage?
Because God said sexual immorality is a shameful act — an evil that must be removed from among the people of Israel. But that law was for the nation of Israel — we must obey the laws of *our* nation (see Deuteronomy 22:21).

God said rapists were to be executed
Deuteronomy 22:25-27 says if a man rapes a woman who is engaged, only the man is to be put to death. The woman is an innocent victim.

Does this mean it's okay to rape a woman who's not engaged? No, of course not. Deuteronomy 22:26 says rape, any rape, is as serious a crime as murder — requiring the death of the rapist.

So, God couldn't possibly be saying a woman has to marry the man who raped her. Why? Because he would be dead, having been executed for raping her.

> But the main reason God wouldn't force a woman to marry the rapist is because God is good (Deuteronomy 32:4). He does not punish women who have been raped.

Why did God make laws for slavery?

In an episode of the TV show *The West Wing,* their fictional U.S. president mockingly tells a Christian he wants to sell his daughter into slavery as sanctioned by Exodus 21:7. Then he oh-so-cleverly asks the Christian what they think would be a good price to get for her. Have you rejected the Bible because of portrayals like this? Did it make you think God is so evil that maybe He's okay with an addict letting men have sex with their child in exchange for drugs? Exodus 21:7 *does* say a man could sell his daughter. Do you want to know why God said that?

There are places in the world where people are so poor and feel so hopeless, they actually sell their children. Those children are then used for child prostitution — sexual slavery. And it's precisely because of people doing those kinds of incredibly evil things that God made laws for slavery. God permitted a man to "sell" his daughter rather than watch her starve to death. But God made rules so it would be done decently, in order to prevent sexual slavery.

Why didn't God just condemn slavery?
God allowed slavery as a necessary evil. A lot of people would have died of starvation without it. They didn't have soup kitchens, or food stamps, or welfare, or Social Security. But the "slavery" that God allowed to happen in the Bible is *not* the slavery we know — it's *not* the kidnapping of people and slave trading that the world practices.

In fact, God said that anyone in Israel who engaged in the slavery that the world practices was to be punished by death (Exodus 21:16; Deuteronomy 24:7; 1 Timothy 1:10).

God is no more okay with slavery than He is with us poking out each other's eyes and teeth (Exodus 21:24). God made laws about "an eye for an eye" and "a man selling his daughter" not because God is evil, as some would have you believe. God made those laws to have mercy shown to the poor, and to prevent the innocent from becoming victims of people's unimaginable evil.

Some people ridicule God because He said "an eye for an eye." But it's not literal. It's a saying which is intended to teach us that the punishment must fit the crime. It means if someone injures you, you can't retaliate by killing his family. God said "an eye for an eye" as a way to try and rein in people's evil. God didn't create evil. Evil comes from people's hearts and from the devil.

 Slavery is one of the evil inventions of people's hearts. It wasn't God's idea. *God just tried to make it less brutal* (Leviticus 25:35-55; Mark 7:20-23; 10:5).

Under the harsh prevailing law of the land, the Code of Hammurabi, theft was punished by death. But God's law softened the penalty by only requiring that restitution be made to the victim. And if the thief couldn't pay restitution, they could work off the debt as a "slave." But those who fell into slavery were to be treated humanely. (Exodus 21:7-11; 22:1-3; Leviticus 25:43; Deuteronomy 4:8)

Slaves in foreign nations were treated with hellish cruelty. If a foreign slave escaped and came to Israel, our merciful God told Israel they were *not* to return the slave but treat them well. God's love and compassion for all people is shown in Deuteronomy 10:16-20, 23:15-16, 24:10-22, and Jonah 4:10-11.

Why didn't Jesus free the slaves?

Jesus didn't come to free the slaves, or kill the rapists, or fix the economy, or end war. Jesus came to walk among us for one supremely important reason: to free us from slavery to sin and save our souls from hell. Jesus frees those held in bondage by the devil and by false teachers, and gives them eternal life (Luke 4:18; 13:10-17; John 3:16; 8:31-36).

Did God harden Pharaoh's heart, and then punish Pharaoh for having a hard heart?

God said to Moses, "I will harden Pharaoh's heart" (Exodus 4:21). Then, when Pharaoh did evil because of his hard heart, God punished Pharaoh for having a hard heart and doing evil. Did God deal Pharaoh a bad hand? (Exodus 7:14-11:10; 12:30; 14:18-31).

Pharaoh hardened his own heart. When God told Moses, "I will harden Pharaoh's heart," God was speaking in a way that would have been familiar to Moses. God said *He* was doing something because He was *letting* someone else do it. Jesus said He did not come to bring peace but war. He meant Christians will have family members who will wage war against them because they're Christians. Jesus will not *make* them wage war — they will *choose* to (Matthew 10:34).

 And God didn't *make* Pharaoh harden his heart —
God let Pharaoh choose to harden his own heart.

God didn't want the Egyptians to sin. God wanted Pharaoh and the Egyptians to turn to Him for salvation. He used their hard hearts and wrongdoing as an opportunity. God punished them to show that He is the one true living God, and that the animal gods they worshipped were nothing. God showed them His power and glory. And God showed them how much He loves those who love Him, by the great lengths He went to in delivering His people, Israel (Deuteronomy 7:6-9; Ezekiel 33:11; Romans 9:17).

Every one of us has two choices. The Bible warns that when we feel like doing evil, we must never say that God is tempting us to do evil. God can never be tempted to do evil and He never tempts anyone to do evil (James 1:13). We can either show our gratitude to God for His patience and forbearance by pursuing His ways, with the free will, abilities, and time He has given us — or we can use God's mercy and grace as an opportunity to indulge in evil things. (Romans 2:4-8; 2 Peter 3:9)

Does God punish families with a generational curse?

There seems to be no end to the ways swindlers will use the Bible to trick people into sending them money. Some claim that God has shown them something in the Bible that no one else has found: "The secret that will free you from a generational curse." They can barely contain themselves trying to impress upon you the urgency of this moment. You must act *now* they say, because God will close this window of opportunity very soon. And you know, they're only telling you this because they care about you.

Deliverance for only $29.95

Of course the only way you can learn the secret is to buy their DVD for $29.95. And those hucksters subliminally imply that the secret will work better if you also buy their useless trinkets and decimate your finances sending them money to support their "work."

God does not contradict Himself

The "generational curse" con men point to Exodus 34:7, where God said He will inflict the punishment for the sins of a father upon his children to the third and fourth generation.

But in Ezekiel 18:20, God said that a son will *not* be punished for the sins of his father, and a father will *not* be punished for the sins of his son. How do we explain this seeming contradiction?

Only those who hate God

The answer is in Exodus 20:5, where God said, "I will inflict the punishment for the sins of a father upon his children to the third and fourth generation *of those who hate Me*."

Yes, of course God inflicts the punishment for the sins of a father onto his children if they hate God and commit the same sins as their father. Don't listen to hucksters. Go to God, He really does love you (John 3:16).

Are all sins equal in God's eyes?

A man is convicted of first-degree murder. He turns to the judge and says: "Judge, I earnestly beseech you: at this very moment, there are scores of people jaywalking in Harvard Square — have mercy on me!" And the judge replies, "You're absolutely right! I'm overturning your conviction, you're free to go." Absurd, right?

Murder vs. Mixed Fabrics

Let's imagine another absurdity: a person comes up to me on the street and says, "Bruce, how can you say it's wrong for me to be a murderer when you're wearing a shirt made of mixed fabrics?" They're mad at me for speaking the truth, that in the Bible God says murder is a wicked sin worthy of the death penalty (Leviticus 24:17).

Murder vs. Hypocrisy

They decide the thing to do is to expose me as a hypocrite for disobeying Leviticus 19:19, which basically says, "Don't wear a shirt made of mixed fabrics." But even if I *were* a hypocrite, how would *that* make it okay to be a murderer? I can just see the news report: "After a 2,000 year silence, God announced today that because one million hypocritical Christians are wearing shirts made of mixed fabrics — murder is no longer a sin." *Not gonna happen!*

All laws are not equal

Some of God's laws are about serious offenses, some are practical, some are about social interactions, and some are symbolic. The law prohibiting a garment of mixed fabrics might have been given for health reasons, or it might have a symbolic meaning of not mixing spiritual with earthly.

Wearing mixed fabrics is not called a detestable act and it is not a capital crime. But those who committed murder were to be executed. All sins are *not* equal in God's eyes.
(Exodus 22:1; Proverbs 6:30-32)

Do all roads lead to God?

Suppose your friend Nick tells you his wife is pregnant. But then Nick's father says Nick's wife is *not* pregnant. So you go back to Nick and tell him what his father said, and Nick says, "He has his truth and I have mine."

Suppose Nick tells you he's going to heaven because he worships Steve. But Nick's father says the only way a person can get to heaven is through Jesus. So you go back to Nick and tell him what his father said, and again Nick says, "He has his truth and I have mine."

Nick cares more about keeping the peace than he cares about truth. But Jesus is not like Nick. Jesus said:

> "Don't think that I have come to bring peace to the earth.
> I have not come to bring peace — but a sword!
> I have come to set a man against his father,
> and a daughter against her mother,
> and a daughter-in-law against her mother-in-law.
> The people living in a man's own house will be his enemies."
>
> — Matthew 10:34-36

Jesus cares more about truth than He does about keeping the peace, because how a person gets to heaven is a matter of life and death.

The matter of Nick's wife can be resolved by a pregnancy test. I can't *prove* to you that the only way a person can get to heaven is through Jesus, but I *can* tell you that Steve and Jesus can't both be the way. Here's why:

 Jesus said you either go through Him — or you won't make it. Jesus made it clear that *He* is the only way to heaven (John 14:6). And if Jesus *is* the only way, that means Steve *can't* get you to heaven.

But Steve said he *can* get you to heaven. Jesus and Steve can't both be correct. That's why they can't coexist. That's why Jesus said He doesn't bring peace, but a sword — it's because people who think Steve is just as good as Jesus will call Christians arrogant and divisive for saying that Jesus is the only way (John 15:18-21).

But Jesus *is* the only way, because only Jesus could solve the problem of sin — our sin. Sin is the breaking of God's laws. It makes God angry. God will judge sinners to eternal damnation. But God doesn't want to do that. Why? Because He loves every one of us. So He was born into a flesh body like ours. In that flesh body He took the punishment and death for our sins (Psalm 7:11; John 3:16).

Jesus rose from the dead three days later
— that's something Steve can't do.
(1 Corinthians 15:1-4)

The only way you can get to heaven is by going through Jesus Christ (John 8:24). All roads do *not* lead to God.

Chapter Four

The Bible

Your Word is a lamp for my feet,
and a light for my path.

- Psalm 119:105

Why are some things in the Bible hard to understand?

The Bible has figures of speech like the ocean has fish.

Some things in the Bible are literal and some are figures of speech. "Literal" follows the rules, but in a "figure of speech" anything goes.

Jesus used figures of speech to temporarily step outside the bounds of reality in order to make a very real point. For instance, Jesus said that when He returns at the second advent, He will come as a thief. But Jesus isn't going to steal your stuff. The only thing Jesus *will* be stealing is the devil's weapons. Jesus compared Himself to a thief in only one way — that He will come at a time when you're not expecting Him. So be alert, be watching (Matthew 24:42-44; Luke 11:21-22; Ephesians 6:11; Revelation 16:15).

Can you tell if this next saying of Jesus is literal or a figure of speech? In John 6:53, Jesus said, "Unless you eat My flesh and drink My blood you will not have eternal life." You're thinking, *Common sense tells me that can't possibly be literal.* But we can't interpret the sayings of Jesus solely by common sense. We need more. We have to search through the Bible.

God said we must never eat blood (Genesis 9:4). And God said we must never murder a human being (Genesis 9:5-6). Killing someone so we could eat them would be murder. But what if the person's already dead, then could we eat them? God said anyone who touches a dead human body is unclean for seven days (Numbers 19:11). That would rule out eating them. Looking at the evidence, we can conclude that Jesus was using a figure of speech because Jesus wouldn't tell us to do something that goes against God's law. But He did get your attention though, didn't He? (Matthew 5:17-19).

That saying of Jesus causes different reactions in people. Some get it, and want to follow Jesus and hear more. But others say, "That's too much for me, I'm not eating flesh, I'm out of here."

 And that's one reason why Jesus used figures of speech — *to strike our minds, move our hearts, and get us to act* — one way or the other (John 6:60-69; Revelation 3:15).

We eat the flesh of Jesus and drink His blood when we accept and receive His sacrifice. Jesus gave His flesh and shed His blood in order to give us eternal life (Mark 14:22-24; John 6:51; 1 Corinthians 10:16).

In Matthew 13:10, the disciples asked Jesus why He spoke to the people in parables — a parable is a type of figure of speech. Jesus told the disciples that God was letting *them* know about the heavenly truths of salvation provided through Jesus Christ, but He wasn't letting the people know. Why did God give truths to the disciples but not to the people? Because the people didn't want them; the people closed their eyes and blocked their ears (Matthew 13:15).

That's another reason why Jesus taught using figures of speech. Jesus didn't give precious things to those who didn't want them (Matthew 11:25-26; 13:10-17; Mark 4:33-34).

Using figures of speech was one of the ways Jesus found out who wanted the truth and was willing to seek it. It showed Him who was hostile, just pretending, apathetic, or too lazy to dig for the truth.

If we don't study the figures of speech in the Bible, we risk falling into confusion, and could be misled by false teachers and cults (Hebrews 11:6).

Why do people say the Bible has contradictions?

Sometimes I'd ask a woman at the Quiz, "If I told you to fall in love with the next man you see, could you do it?" The answer of course is no. She feels nothing for him — he's just some guy, a stranger. Her heart is closed to him. It's the same with the Bible. Until something happens in your heart, you'll see the Bible as strange, impossible to understand, and contradictory.

Some people want an excuse to reject the Bible

Jesus said it's because they've made the decision to close their eyes, block their ears, and harden their heart (Matthew 13:9-17).

If you *do* want to understand the Bible, come humbly and sincerely, with respect and a contrite heart. Then study, ask, and seek — diligently. As you study the Bible with that heart, God will lead you to the answers. You'll find that the things you thought were contradictions are perfectly compatible truths (Psalm 51:17; Proverbs 1:1-7; Matthew 7:7-18; Hebrews 11:6; James 1:5-7).

The light and the lights

Let me show you how to study by digging into a couple of alleged contradictions. For those who feel hostility to God or aren't dedicated students of the Bible, the introduction of light in the first chapter of Genesis can elicit a cry of "contradiction!" Why, they wonder, do verses 3-5 say there was light, when the sun and the moon weren't created until verses 14-18?

In Genesis 1:2, darkness covered the waters of the earth. Then the Spirit of God moved upon the waters and God said: "Let there be light." *That light is God's Spirit.* The Spirit of God is not created, but has always been and always will be. God's Spirit is warmth and goodness, opposed to the evil darkness of the devil (Genesis 1:3; John 1:5; 3:19-21; 8:12; 2 Corinthians 4:6; 1 John 1:5; Revelation 21:23; 22:5).

In Genesis 1:5, the light of God's Spirit is given the name
"Day" and the darkness of the devil's evil is called "Night."
These are not the day and night which came about when
God created the sun and the moon in Genesis 1:14-18.
No contradiction — only beautiful truth.

Did James contradict Paul?

The apostle Paul said God will not consider anyone to be saved
because they performed works. He concluded that a person is saved
by faith, without doing works (Romans 3:28). And in Romans 5:1,
Paul wrote that we have made peace with God because we've been
made right in His eyes through our faith in the Lord Jesus Christ.

So why would James write that a person is saved by works, and not
only by believing? James said that believing without performing
works is a faith which is dead — as dead as a person's body after
the spirit has departed (James 2:24-26).

Is it a contradiction? No, of course not. It's elementary, my dear
reader. They are two sides of one coin. Paul is making the point that
Jesus earned our salvation and gives it to us as a free gift which we
receive only through our faith. James is *not* disagreeing with Paul
that salvation comes only through our faith.

 James is making the point that *our faith must be*
accompanied by works in order to prove that it's genuine faith
(Matthew 7:21; Luke 6:46-49; 14:25-35).

So you see then, by engaging in honest Bible study, what seemed
like contradictions will be revealed as glorious truths. If you think
there's a contradiction, do yourself a favor: dig into the Bible and
find the explanation.

How can I tell true Bible teachings from false?

How can you tell true from false? Take a lesson from the bank teller, who can instantly tell a counterfeit bill by the way it feels. That's because they're so familiar with what a real bill feels like — *from constantly handling real bills.*

This is an urgent warning

There are people who say they are teaching truth from the Bible, but God *did not* send them. Some of them want money and power, some are on an ego trip, others are just ignorant (2 Peter 2:1-3; 3:16). They're selling a counterfeit product that in some ways resembles the real thing, or what people think is the real thing. But their product is poison and it results in a large number of deaths — spiritually.

The apostle Peter told us to crave *the pure milk* of the Bible (1 Peter 2:2). A nursing mother is a fitting symbol of pure nourishment. And there's so much meaning in Peter's expression "the pure milk" which he used to describe the Bible. It means sincere and innocent. It means it's not a trick, not a lie. And it means that nothing has been added.

What if you poured dirt into a glass of milk?

Even though there's milk in there, if you have a steady diet of milk mixed with dirt you'll get sick and eventually die. That's what false teachers give you when they add their own teachings and rules to the pure milk of God's Word.

When Jesus walked the earth, there were some so-called spiritual authorities called Pharisees. They were greedy, proud, and self-righteous hypocrites. They exploited the people, held power over them, and didn't care about their spiritual well-being.

The Pharisees added their own rules to God's commandments, but Jesus shone a light on them so everyone could see their wickedness. While a crowd of people listened, Jesus told the Pharisees that because they were adding their own teachings to the Bible, they were emptying the Bible of its power to save. Jesus told those religious leaders they would be very sorry one day. He accused them of taking away the key to heaven — the knowledge of how a person gets there. Jesus said it's like they put heaven out of business and chained the door. Their religion was poison (Matthew 23:13; Mark 7:13; Luke 11:52).

You've heard people say they're "saved." It means they've been *saved from eternal death* and will be immortal because they put their faith in the gospel, the sacrificial death of Jesus for their sins. (1 Corinthians 15:1-4)

We're saved by God's grace, which we receive through our faith
How do we get faith? By hearing the Word of God, the Bible. Only the true Word from the Bible can give you saving faith. If you have the counterfeit, then you're drinking death (Romans 10:17; Ephesians 2:8).

 So you've got to be constantly handling the Bible, becoming so familiar with the Bible — the real, the true — that you'll be able to instantly recognize the counterfeit.

That's why Jesus said, "Come," "Take," "Learn," (Matthew 11:28-29). It means you have to get up, go to Him, take His Word, carry it with you everywhere you go, open it up, and study it so you can learn about Him (Deuteronomy 6:6-9).

Jesus will deliver you and protect you from false spiritual authorities. Stay with Jesus, drink only the pure milk of God's Word, and ask God to give you the ability to tell true from false (Luke 4:18; John 8:31-32; Acts 17:11; 2 Corinthians 3:17; 2 Timothy 2:15).

If someone tells me there's another Bible, should I believe them?

What if someone has "another Bible"? They tell you God revealed it to a prophet, a person who speaks for Him. Or they say an angel of the Lord came from God and delivered it. They claim it's a companion edition or a sequel to the Bible. They might tell you the Bible we have now is corrupted, or that God changed His mind and in this new book God is telling us the latest, most up-to-date information. Should you believe them? If it *is* from God, you don't want to miss out and risk disobeying God. But how do you know if it's real?

God made an example of a "man of God" to teach us what to do if someone tells us they have another Bible. God told the man of God to deliver a message, and gave him instructions that afterwards he was to come right back and not stop to eat or drink. But on the way back a prophet came to the man of God and said, "An angel told me to tell you that God wants you to come to my house to eat." But the prophet was lying. The man of God believed him, though, and went to his house to eat. And God killed the man of God because he listened to a lie instead of obeying the word of God (1 Kings 13:1-34).

There is not another Bible
Even if they use the name Jesus or claim to respect Him — "another Bible" does not come from God. By killing the man of God's physical body, God warned us that if we receive another Bible we will suffer the death of our soul.

 Jude 1:3 refers to "the faith once delivered." "The faith" is the Christian faith found in the Bible. The word "once" is the same Greek word used to say that Jesus was crucified "once" (Hebrews 9:28). The crucifixion of Jesus paid for sin completely. Jesus never has to be crucified again. And in the Bible, God told us *everything* we need to know. God gave us the Bible, once and for all, so we wouldn't be controlled by men, or worse, by the devil (Galatians 1:6-9; 2 John 1:10-11).

How old is the earth according to the Bible?

Many Christians say the earth is 6,000 years old. Is that what the Bible says? From Adam to Christ is about 4,000 years, and from Christ to the present is about 2,000. But did something happen between the time God created the earth and when He created Adam?

We all know what the first two verses of the Bible say:

> In the beginning God created the heavens and the earth.
> And the earth was a chaotic wasteland, and empty.
>
> - Genesis 1:1-2

But did God *create* the earth as a chaotic wasteland? In the original Hebrew, the expression "chaotic wasteland" is the word *tohu*. In Isaiah 45:18, God said He did *not* create the earth as a chaotic wasteland (*tohu*) — He created it as a place suitable to sustain life.

If Genesis 1:2 says God created the earth as a chaotic wasteland and Isaiah 45:18 says God did *not* create the earth as a chaotic wasteland, then that would be a contradiction. But the Bible does not contradict itself. So why does Genesis 1:2 say the earth *was* a chaotic wasteland? The word "was" is the same Hebrew word, *hayah*, used in Genesis 19:26 to say that Lot's wife *became* a pillar of salt.

 The answer is: God created the earth suitable to sustain life. God did not create the earth *tohu*, and why would He? But then later it *became* a chaotic wasteland. Why did the earth become a chaotic wasteland? God destroyed the earth after Lucifer rebelled (Isaiah 14:12-20; Jeremiah 4:23-27). And then God *recreated* the earth when He created Adam. God made the earth anew (Genesis 1:2b). So there was a period of time from when God created the earth and when He recreated it. Therefore the Bible is not incompatible with science which says the earth is billions of years old.

Is the theory of evolution compatible with the Bible?

Some politicians and religious leaders try not to offend anybody. They say they believe God created life but He did it through evolution. But that's impossible.

God's account of creation in the Holy Bible and Darwin's theory of evolution cannot both be true. Do you know which one is absolutely true and which one is absolutely false? Hint: Darwin's theory is anti-God.

The original, complete title of Darwin's first famous book is:

On the Origin of Species by Means of Natural Selection or the <u>Preservation of Favored Races</u> in the Struggle for Life

In his subsequent book *The Descent of Man*, Darwin wrote about the human race much more than in the *Origin of Species*. Here is a quote from the "Races of Man" chapter:

"Whether primeval man, when he possessed but few arts, and those of the rudest kind, and when his power of language was extremely imperfect, would have deserved to be called man, must depend on the definition which we employ. <u>In a series of forms graduating insensibly from some ape-like creature to man as he now exists,</u> it would be impossible to fix on any definite point when the term 'man' ought to be used."

Darwin's theory of evolution portrays humans as evolved from ape-like creatures and divided into different "races." Of course Darwin considered his own white race to be the most evolved. Darwin's theory has been appropriated to support racist ideologies and organizations. That kind of thinking, seeing some people as inferior, has led to all kinds of evils.

But God's Word, the Bible, tells us what really happened. God created human beings in His image. We didn't "evolve" from lower life forms. Darwin's theory of evolution requires there to be different kinds of humans. But the Bible tells us that God only made one kind of human. There's only one race, the human race (Genesis 9:6; Mark 10:6).

 It's heartless and cruel to teach children that they evolved from lower life forms akin to apes rather than having been created in the image of a Heavenly Father who cares about them. Darwinism relegates us to a type of animal, taking away from the preciousness of every human life.

As far as God's loving offer of salvation goes, all people are equal. God is not a respecter of persons. Jesus Christ died on a cross for the whole world, for every person, because He loves every person. (Mark 16:15; Romans 10:11-13; 1 John 2:2; Revelation 5:9)

Where did Cain's wife come from?

In 1925, in what became known as the "Scopes Monkey Trial," school-teacher John Scopes was tried for defying a Tennessee law which banned the teaching of Darwin's theory of evolution in public schools.

At one point in the trial, defense attorney Clarence Darrow asked the prosecutor— William Jennings Bryant, a Christian— to testify as an expert in the Bible. Darrow asked Bryant to explain how Cain took a wife in Genesis 4:17, when according to the Bible the only people on the planet were Cain, his father Adam, and his mother Eve. As Darrow expected, Bryant was unable to answer the question. Darrow cited this as proof that the Bible was flawed and less trustworthy than Darwin's theory of evolution.

Is the Bible untrustworthy?

Some ask, "If you don't know where Cain's wife came from, how can you be sure about anything in the Bible?" God didn't tell us where Cain's wife came from. That doesn't mean the Bible is flawed or un-trustworthy. God told us in the Bible what we need to know about sin and salvation, and He expects us to learn it and obey it. And we also learn from the Bible that Darwin's theory of evolution is incorrect and anti-God — because God *did* tell us that He created *all* the different kinds of living beings, in Genesis, chapters 1 and 2.

Where *could* Cain's wife have come from?

Genesis 5:4 tells us that Adam and Eve had daughters. So, some conclude that Cain must have married one of them. Another possibility is that there were people, civilizations, in existence before Adam and Eve were created, and Cain married one of them. How could that be? Some believe that in Genesis 1:26, God created "mankind," the people who populated the world. Then later, in Genesis 2:7, God created one man, Adam, from whom came Eve, and placed them in the Garden of Eden (Genesis 2:8, 22).

How could polar bears live on the ark?

Skeptics often ask me this and other questions
such as,
"What did the lions eat on the ark?"
or
"Why didn't the lions eat Noah?"
Believers also wonder about things like that.
Everything recorded in the Bible is accurate and true.
If something seems to be impossible or a contradiction,
it's not — you just need more information.

Do you believe God can do anything?
It was God who led all the animals onto the ark, not Noah. Our God,
who created the sun and gives us eyesight — He could lead all the
creatures onto Noah's ark and make it work. Yes; zebras, bats, insects,
even lions, whatever He wanted (Genesis 7:9, 13-16).

 God didn't tell us how He did it.
You either choose to believe it or you don't.

God protected Daniel from the lions
When Daniel was put into a cage full of lions and left there all night,
God protected him. The lions didn't touch Him. God is amazing: He
will even make lions eat straw (Isaiah 11:7; Daniel 6:16-23; Luke 1:37).

Chapter Five

Who is Jesus Christ?

What I've discovered is that to learn the teachings of Christ,
and to grow in my relationship with Him, is the most valuable
thing there is. In comparison, all the things the world values are
a bad deal. I've made the best deal — I've thrown out the world's
valuables as though they are garbage so that I can have Christ instead.

- the apostle Paul, Philippians 3:8

Jesus Christ is the most famous, most important person who ever walked the earth and the most misunderstood. Now is the time to start learning who Jesus is. You might be surprised by what you discover.

Who is Jesus?

Jesus Christ is our Redeemer

Long before Food Stamps and Unemployment Insurance, if a person went broke they might have resorted to selling themselves into slavery.

But God commanded that in the nation of Israel, every family was to have a man who would help relatives who were in need. He was called a kinsman redeemer. If a relative sold themselves into slavery, the kinsman redeemer could pay money to buy them back — to regain their freedom — to redeem them (Leviticus 25:47-49).

And God used that Old Testament law of the kinsman redeemer to teach us about someone who would walk the earth 1,500 years later — *our* Kinsman Redeemer, Jesus Christ.

Question: the Old Testament kinsman redeemer bought back his family member from slavery. Why would I need Jesus to redeem me? I'm not a slave.

> Well actually, all of us sold ourselves into slavery to
> sinful disobedience, which results in the death of our soul.
> Jesus came to redeem our souls from our slavery to sin
> (Proverbs 5:22; Isaiah 47:4; Romans 6:16-23; 2 Timothy 2:26).

But the Bible tells us that our souls can't be redeemed with money or with any of the valuable things of the earth — things that last for a while but then rot and decay. In fact, all the money in the world isn't enough to redeem a person's soul (Psalm 49:7-9,15; 1 Peter 1:18). Then how did Jesus redeem us? We have to once again look at a law that was commanded by God in the Old Testament:

> If anyone in Israel eats blood, then I will set My face against
> that person, and I will remove them from My people, because
> the life of the body is in the blood. And I am letting you bring
> blood to the altar, so you can appease Me and preserve your
> life.   - Leviticus 17:10-11

God used blood as the symbol for death in order to get our attention.
The sight of blood sends chills up our spine. Killing an animal and
bringing its blood to the altar gave the children of Israel a stark
illustration. They began to understand the supreme majesty of God's
holiness and justice system. They learned that death is the price we
pay for disobeying God. But it gave them just a temporary reprieve
because, as the Bible tells us, the blood of animals can't make a full
payment for sin. The blood of animals can't redeem our soul.
(Romans 3:22-26; 5:8-10; Hebrews 10:1-10)

All through the Old Testament, God gave us many laws, events, and
even people which bear a similarity to the one that the whole Bible
leads us to — Jesus Christ.

 The futile shedding of animal blood was meant to point
people to Jesus Christ. Because only the precious blood of
Jesus could satisfy God as the full payment for all our sins.
Why? Because Jesus Christ is the only sinless one.

The blood of Jesus is special. His blood buys us eternal life. Jesus is
God with us, God in the flesh, God our Savior (Hebrews 9:11-28; 1 Peter
1:19-20; Revelation 1:5; compare Exodus 24:3-8 with Mark 14:23-24).

When you get tired of being held as a slave to sin, Jesus is there for
you. He wants to be your Kinsman Redeemer. Jesus says that if you
seek Him you will find Him (Matthew 7:7-8).

> *You shall seek Me, and find Me,*
> *when you search for Me with all your heart.*
>
>   - Jeremiah 29:13

Was Jesus just a man?

If your Jesus is just a man, then your Jesus is a lie, he's a fraud, an impostor. You are doomed, you will die in your sins, because your Jesus can't save anybody!

Jesus said: "Before Abraham was, I Am." *And* Jesus said: "You will die in your sins if you do not believe that I Am" (John 8:24,58).

When wicked men came to arrest Jesus on false charges, Jesus said to them, "Who are you looking for?"
They said, "We're looking for Jesus of Nazareth."
And Jesus said, "I Am." When Jesus said, "I Am," all of those wicked men went backwards and fell to the ground (John 18:6).

Now you might be wondering, what does *that* prove? You don't see the big deal. Well, let me tell you who *did* see it as a big deal — the Judaists who heard Jesus say those things. They saw it as a very big deal, as you can see from the following account:

> The Judaists picked up stones to kill Jesus.
> And Jesus said to them, "At My Father's direction I have done many good works. For which of those works are you going to kill Me?"
> They replied, "We're not stoning You to death because of some good work that You've done. We're stoning You for blaspheming God! Because You are a man, and You're claiming that You are God."   - John 10:31-33

"We're stoning You for blaspheming God! Because You are a man, and You're claiming that You are God."
                                                        - John 10:33

In the book of Exodus, God appeared to Moses in a burning bush and told him to go to the children of Israel to deliver them from bondage in Egypt. Moses asked God: "When I say to the children of Israel, 'The God of your fathers has sent me,' and they say to me, 'What is His name?' what shall I say?"

And God said to Moses:"Tell them I Am has sent you" (Exodus 3:13-14).

 "I Am" is the Sacred Name of God. When Jesus says He is "I Am," Jesus is telling us that He is God.

You still don't see it? Well, I have to tell you that the reason you don't see it is because you've chosen to harden your heart against God. And I could try to talk you into seeing it until I'm blue in the face, but you won't get it until *you* change your mind (Matthew 13:15).

If you deny that Jesus is God, you reject the Bible and Christianity. You're denying God Himself. You'll have nothing: no salvation, no God. You'll be like the people popping up on street corners everywhere who deny that Jesus is God. They are enemies of Christ. (1 John 2:22-26; 4:1-3; 2 John 1:6-11)

The Bible is crystal clear, from beginning to end, that Jesus Christ is God. Study it!

In Isaiah 43:11, God said:

> "I am the LORD, and there is no Savior besides Me."

And Titus 2:13 says:

> "We are waiting in joyful expectation for the appearing of the glory of our great God and Savior — Jesus Christ."

How can Jesus be both God and the Son of God?

First, a question: What was Jesus' father's name?

When the angel Gabriel told a virgin named Mary that God's Son would be conceived in her womb, she responded, "How can that be? I'm not physically intimate with a man." Jesus was not the result of a physical union (contrary to one cult's science fiction story). Mary's future husband, Joseph, had nothing to do with it. Joseph was the father of Jesus only in his role as legal guardian when Jesus was a child. Jesus was conceived in Mary's womb by the power of God's Holy Spirit. That's beyond our understanding. But it means that God is the Father of Jesus (Luke 1:34-35; 2:48-51).

When we say, "Jesus is the Son of God" it means "Jesus is God"
God is Spirit, so we can't see Him. But God came and showed Himself to us. That's who Jesus is — God showing us God. Jesus is God, in person (you could say, "in the flesh") explaining God to us.
(Deuteronomy 18:15-19; Matthew 1:23; John 1:1,18; 4:24; 10:30-33; 14:9; Colossians 2:9; Hebrews 1:8)

No, that doesn't make two Gods
Many Christians create confusion by using the expression "the three persons of the trinity." They might be trying to make the point that God's Holy Spirit is not some kind of impersonal force as some falsely teach. But God is not three persons. God is one person. And no, I don't believe in that ridiculous teaching called *modalism*, the belief that Jesus and the Holy Spirit have not existed eternally, but are just temporary modes of operation that God assumes when needed. Naturally, God *always* has His thoughts and Spirit.
(John 1:1-4,14; 6:62; 17:5; 2 Corinthians 3:17; Colossians 1:17)

I'm going to explain the Son of God clearly, step by step
Not two Gods, but one God in two places at the same time:

1) God created the universe and established laws. Then He put humans in flesh bodies, placed us on earth, and gave us free will to choose whether or not to obey His laws. We chose to disobey. That's why we all die. But that's just part one of the penalty. The second is the death of the soul, when a person ceases to exist (Matthew 10:28).

2) God loves every one of us. He doesn't want us to cease to exist. So He had a plan, a way we could avoid perishing forever. (John 3:16; 10:11-18; 15:13; Romans 5:8; 1 John 4:8-10)

3) God required that for us to be delivered from eternal death, a sacrifice had to be made, and the one sacrificed had to be one who never broke any of God's laws. This meant there was no one on earth who could save us because everyone breaks God's laws. It meant that only God Himself could provide the sacrifice (Genesis 22:8).

4) But God required that because humans break God's laws in flesh bodies, the sacrifice for sin had to be made in a flesh body. The person who would be the sacrifice would shed their blood, be killed (Philippians 2:5-11; Hebrews 9:26).

5) That's why God Himself had to be born in the womb of a virgin, live a life without breaking any laws, be executed on false charges, and then rise from the dead three days later (Matthew 1:21).

 Can God die?
No, God can't die. But, can God come and be born in a human body so He can die? Yes. That's why Jesus is both God and God's Son. There's no salvation without God's Son (John 1:14; 3:14-18,36; 8:24; 14:6; Acts 4:10-12; Titus 2:13; 1 John 2:22-23).

You can't just order God to explain the Son of God to you
You must come to God with the right heart. The Bible teaches that a healthy fear of God is the first step to knowledge. Fools despise wisdom and instruction, but a good understanding is had by all those who respect God (Psalm 111:10; Proverbs 1:7; John 7:17; 8:43; 1 Corinthians 2:14).

Did Jesus treat women fairly?

Men and their religions tend to treat women cruelly.
But not Jesus. He is the great liberator of women.

Jesus is the best thing to happen to women. He brought a new, radical idea — that women are to be treated with dignity. Jesus treated women with respect — He took them seriously. He did not see them as inferior to men, either intellectually or spiritually. And Jesus defended women from rude and ignorant men (Matthew 19:1-9; Mark 14:1-6; Luke 7:36-50).

When Jesus encountered a woman caught in adultery, He rescued the woman, spoke truth to her, and invited her to repent. Jesus saves sinners (John 8:1-11).

And Jesus frees women. One day, Jesus was teaching in one of the local places of worship. He noticed a woman, a member of that congregation. She'd had a spirit of infirmity for eighteen years. She was bent over and couldn't lift herself up at all (Luke 13:10-17).

Jesus called her to Him and said, "Woman, you are loosed from your infirmity." Then Jesus laid His hands on her and immediately she stood up straight again, and she glorified God (Isaiah 42:16; 61:1).

But the leader of her congregation didn't glorify God, and he didn't thank Jesus for healing the woman. No, instead, he burned with anger and rebuked Jesus. He told Jesus that the law of Moses forbids healing people on the holy Sabbath day.

That wasn't true. The law was meant to ban *work* on the Sabbath, so people would have a day to seek God, worshipping Him and studying His Word. Jesus knew that the leaders of this congregation had no problem with unloosing their farm animals on the Sabbath and bringing them to the water hole.

Jesus said, "Why then don't you want this woman, who is a daughter of Abraham and has been bound by Satan for eighteen years, to be loosed on the Sabbath?" When Jesus said that, the leaders of the congregation were ashamed, but all the people rejoiced because of the glorious things Jesus did (Matthew 12:1-8).

God chose a medical doctor to write down the record of this encounter — Luke, the beloved physician (Colossians 4:14).

Luke tells us from the woman's medical history that she had suffered for eighteen years from a condition he calls a spirit of infirmity. This was weakness or frailty. Luke says "she was bent over and couldn't lift herself up at all." But it was because the woman felt unable to lift herself up. Her physical illness was the result of the mental and emotional stress she was under.

 She was all bent over and unable to stand up straight because the leaders of her church put her in that condition by making her feel that she was less valuable than an animal.

> But Jesus paid her the highest honor by calling her a daughter of Abraham, a righteous child of faith, and she stood up straight again to her full height.

Did Jesus try to avoid going to the cross?

Most churches slander Jesus. They teach that Jesus was so scared on the night before He was to be crucified, that He asked God if He could back out.

Jesus *was* hurting

On the night before He was to be crucified, Jesus went with His disciples to the Garden of Gethsemane to pray. When they got there, Jesus was overwhelmed with intense emotional pain. He told the disciples He felt like He was being swallowed up by sadness (Matthew 26:2, 36-38). Then Jesus fell to His knees, with His face to the ground, and Jesus prayed:

> "Oh, My Father, if You can find another way,
>   then take this cup away from Me.
>   But if not, then don't do what I'm asking,
>   do as You have planned."   - Matthew 26:39

And His sweat became as large drops of blood falling to the ground (Luke 22:44).

In their 1968 Classic Rock song *Sympathy For The Devil*, the Rolling Stones sang: "I was 'round when Jesus Christ had his moment of doubt and pain."

The idea that Jesus wanted to back out of the crucifixion has spread from churches into popular culture and is accepted as fact. Churches claim that the human part of Jesus felt fear, which made Jesus want to avoid being crucified. But that's just speculation. There's nothing written in the Bible to document that assertion. So why say it? Why give those who hate Jesus an insult to cast at Him? His enemies will point out all the accounts of people who were 100% human but went to their death bravely, willingly, and honorably. Then they will ask why Jesus was unable to do that (John 11:16).

Then what did Jesus really mean?
Why was Jesus overwhelmed with sadness on the night before He
was to be crucified? And what was the "cup" Jesus asked God to
take from Him?

What do we know about Jesus?
What does the Bible teach us about the character of Jesus? Was He
courageous or was He cowardly? Was He strong or weak? Jesus was
courageous and strong. And what were His most important qualities?
They were mercy, compassion, pity, and self-sacrificing love.
(Mark 10:32-34; Luke 7:11-15; John 2:13-17; Philippians 2:5-8).

Why was Jesus swallowed up in sadness?
Jesus wasn't feeling sorry for Himself. The sadness Jesus felt before
He was crucified was for those He loved, for His people, Israel.
Why was He sad for them? Because He knew the punishment, the
wrath of God, that was going to come upon them for rejecting their
Savior, Jesus Christ. Jesus had compared Himself to a mother hen
who tries to gather her chicks together, but they were unwilling.
Jesus wept for them (Matthew 23:37; Luke 19:41-44).

Which cup?
In the Bible, a cup is used to symbolize someone's fate, what they've
got coming to them. God's judgment is spoken of as being poured
out or drunk from a cup (Psalm 75:8; Ezekiel 23:31; Revelation 14:10).

> The cup Jesus asked God to take from Him was not
> the crucifixion but the *cup of wrath that God would pour
> on the nation of Israel* for rejecting and killing Jesus.

 Jesus went to the cross to save souls. It broke His heart
to know that for some, His crucifixion would mean their
condemnation (1 Timothy 2:3-6; Hebrews 5:8-9).

Did sin touch Jesus?

I often hear someone during a sermon or Bible study say that Jesus became sin or that He took the sin of the world onto His body. They're wrong to say that, and here's why.

As Jesus was dying on the cross, He cried out:

> "My God, my God,
>   why have You forsaken me?"   - Matthew 27:46 (KJV)

But Jesus wasn't speaking to God. Whenever Jesus prayed, He *never* called God "God." Jesus always addressed God as "Father" (Matthew 11:25; Luke 23:34, 46; John 12:28; 17:1).

The words "My God, my God, why have you forsaken me?" were spoken by David, who was king of Israel a thousand years before Jesus walked the earth. They are the first line of Psalm 22. The Gospels of Matthew and Mark record that as He was dying nailed to a cross, Jesus quoted that first line of Psalm 22. And the Gospel of John records that the last words Jesus spoke from the cross before He died were, "It is finished" [Greek: *teleo*]. That's the same thing David wrote as the *last* line of Psalm 22 [Hebrew: *asah*] (John 19:30).

Jesus was *the* teacher. He was always teaching. And He even taught as He was dying on the cross: He taught Psalm 22. Jesus wanted to save those evil people who crucified Him. He hoped they would see that only God Himself could have caused David to write Psalm 22, which described the crucifixion of Jesus and the salvation which would be made available because of it — one thousand years before it happened. Jesus wanted to touch their hearts with God's Word, to lead them to repentance and salvation. Do your own study by comparing Psalm 22:7-8 with Matthew 27:39-43; Psalm 22:16 with John 19:18 and 20:27; Psalm 22:18 with John 19:24.

Most pastors teach that Jesus *did* think God had forsaken Him —
and that God *did* forsake Jesus. Those pastors concoct a monstrous
interpretation to explain why they think Jesus was forsaken by God.

They insult Jesus, claiming that Jesus took the sin of the world on His
body, and make the blasphemous statement that God turned His
back on Jesus *because Jesus became sin*. Those pastors don't understand
two verses:

1) Isaiah 53:12 says that Jesus <u>bare</u> the sin of many (KJV).
But the meaning of "bare" in the original Hebrew is "bare away."
It's used to refer to people who lift up their eyes or lift up their
voice (Genesis 13:10; 21:16).

> Jesus didn't take our sins onto His body —
> He *lifted away* our sins.

2) Second Corinthians 5:21 says that God made Jesus to be <u>sin</u> for
us. The Greek word translated "sin" is *hamartia*. This is exactly the
same word used for "sin offering" in the Book of Leviticus in the
Greek translation of the Old Testament, the Septuagint.

> Jesus didn't become sin — He became the *sin offering,*
> the sinless sacrifice for sin, our Passover Lamb without
> spot or blemish (Exodus:12:5; Isaiah 53:10; 1 Corinthians 5:7;
> Hebrews 7:26; 1 Peter 1:18-19; 1 John 3:5).

 **God didn't forsake Jesus, and God said He won't forsake
His people:**

I will never leave you, nor forsake you.

- Hebrews 13:5

(Deuteronomy 4:31; Romans 8:38-39; John 10:27-29)

Do you believe Jesus rose from the dead?

Someone said to me once, "I'm a Christian, I just don't believe that Jesus literally rose from the dead." Well I've got news for that person — they're not a Christian. Of all the miraculous, mysterious things about the Christian faith, the resurrection of Jesus is the most important. Without the resurrection of Jesus Christ, Christianity would be meaningless. There would be no reason for our hope.

No one can top the surprises that Jesus planned for His friends. Jesus was dead because His enemies had Him unjustly executed. His friends were sad; they thought they'd never see Him again.

You've heard of Mary Magdalene. She was a good woman, a brave woman. Early in the morning before sunrise, Mary went to the tomb where the body of Jesus had been placed. But the door was open. Mary stood outside the tomb, crying. Then as she wept, she stooped down and looked into the tomb. She saw two angels. They were sitting where the body of Jesus had been. The body was gone. The angels asked Mary, "Why are you crying?" And she said, "Because they have taken my Lord. I don't know where they put His body."

As she was saying that, she turned and saw a man standing behind her. The man said to her, "Woman, why are you crying? Who are you looking for?" Mary figured he must be the grounds-keeper of the cemetery, so she said to him, "Sir, if you've moved the body, tell me where you've put Him, and I'll take Him."

While he was standing behind her, the man said, "Mary." Then she knew who it was. Mary turned around and said, "My Teacher." It was Jesus. He had been dead, but now He was alive (John 20:1, 11-16).

Next, Jesus would surprise the disciples. But didn't Jesus tell them that He would die and then rise from the dead? Yes, Jesus *did* tell them, but they hadn't understood (Matthew 16:20-23; Luke 18:31-34).

And Jesus often hid truths in a riddle. One time He said that when the temple gets destroyed, He will rebuild it in three days. The temple Jesus was talking about was His body. Jesus rose again after being dead for three days (John 2:18-22).

When Jesus rose from the dead, He gave Mary Magdalene the honor of being the first person to see Him. And Jesus told Mary to go and tell His disciples that she saw Him, that He was risen from death. She went and told them, but they wouldn't believe her. Later, when Jesus saw the disciples, He was angry with them and told them their hearts were cold because they refused to believe Mary when she told them she saw Jesus alive (Mark 16:9-14).

The disciples were scared. They were afraid that the same people who murdered Jesus would get them too. They were all together, hiding with the doors bolted shut. But suddenly there was a person standing in their midst. They looked, and it was Jesus. Jesus said, "Peace to you" (John 20:19-31) .

The resurrection of Jesus is the greatest surprise ever. It's the most important thing that's ever happened. Without it there would be no Christianity — we would all be doomed. Those who put their trust in Jesus will also rise from the dead, spiritually, in this life. And forever (John 11:25-27; Romans 6:3-5).

 If you don't believe that Jesus actually died and literally resurrected from the dead, and lives forever — then you are not a Christian — you need to repent.
(1 Corinthians 15:1-4; 12-22; 29-32; 53-58)

If Christ was not raised from the dead, then your faith is worthless — you're still in your sins.
                                                    - 1 Corinthians 15:17

But Christ *was* raised and lives forever — Hebrews 7:25; Revelation 1:17-18.

Why is Jesus the only way?

Some time before God placed Adam and Eve in the Garden of Eden, something significant had already happened: one of God's best angels went bad and became the Enemy we know as the devil. God decided He wouldn't kill the devil just yet but would let him live for a while, because the devil could serve some important purposes in God's dealings with people. That's why God let the devil own one of the trees in the Garden of Eden (Genesis 2:9; Isaiah 14:12-20; Ezekiel 28:12-19; 1 Corinthians 5:5).

God made Adam and Eve perfect and holy. Why? Because God is perfect and holy. God told Adam and Eve, "Do not eat from the devil's tree or you will die." But the devil whispered in Eve's ear and seduced her, with the result being that Eve, and then Adam, disobeyed God and ate from the devil's tree. Adam and Eve became criminals and they would have to suffer the penalty — they would have to die. (Genesis 2:17; 3:4-6; Romans 6:23; 1 Peter 1:16)

Later on, God gave us the concept of human government. Our criminal justice system was given to us by God in order to restrain evil so we can live in a peaceful society. When someone breaks the law they are ultimately brought before a judge, who passes sentence on them (Genesis 9:6; Romans 13:1-5) .

But what would happen if the judge let them go free?
God said:

> A judge who says to the wicked, "You are innocent,"
> will be cursed by many people and denounced by the nations.
> - Proverbs 24:24

That's right, the *judge himself* would now be guilty of a crime and be subject to punishment. And if God let Adam and Eve go free, then *God Himself* would be unjust.

"But I didn't eat from the devil's tree — why do I have to die?"

Even if we've never been in trouble with the police, every single one of us is a criminal. We have broken the law, God's perfect law, and so we too have to die; and not just our physical body, but our soul also must die. We will be blotted out as though we never existed. It has to be that way because God's justice system is perfect (Isaiah 61:8; Matthew 10:28; Romans 3:23; 5:12; 6:23).

"But why didn't anybody tell me?"

God says He *is* telling everyone. He gave us this universe, His marvelous creation, and He gave us a conscience. And He has given us the Bible, and a brain which He expects us to use (Joshua 1:8; Matthew 4:4; Acts 17:11; Romans 1:18-20; 2:14-15).

But God loves us. He made a way to save us so we can live forever. And God showed us what was required to save us in a symbol, in the Passover lamb which had to be "without blemish" (Exodus 12:5).

 It means that the Savior who shed His blood in our place had to be *sinless*. Therefore, only God could save us because only God is sinless. That's why Jesus Christ, who is "God with us," is the only way.

(Isaiah 7:14; 43:11; Matthew 1:21-23; John 11:25-27; 1 Peter 1:18-19; 2:22; 1 John 3:5)

Chapter Six

The
Holy Spirit

When God gives you His Holy Spirit
He pours His love into your heart.

- Romans 5:5

From the time Jesus left Earth until the time He returns, God is present with believers by living inside them as the Holy Spirit. Believers cultivate their relationship with the Holy Spirit by making the Bible their constant companion.

What's the Holy Spirit?

God used a street preacher named Tilman to get me into the Bible. One day Tilman asked me, "Do you have the Holy Spirit?" I said, "What's the Holy Spirit?" Now that I have the Holy Spirit and the Bible, I look back and realize how empty my life was before. You might be thinking, "Of course your life was empty, Bruce, you were a loser." Yes you're right, I was a loser. But there are (and have been) millions of Christians who aren't losers in this world. They're scholars, university professors, scientists, professional athletes, successful business owners, members of the military and law enforcement, and on and on. And they, too, will tell you that their lives were empty before they had the Holy Spirit and the Bible.

How many Gods do Christians have?

I think many Christians imagine their arrival in heaven will go something like this: They'll be met at the door, welcomed in, and their greeter will say, "I'd like you to meet Jesus." After Jesus hugs and kisses them, the greeter says, "Come this way and I'll introduce you to the Father, and then we'll go up to the third floor so you can meet the Holy Spirit." Is that how it will be? No. The Holy Spirit is not "the third member of the trinity" as many Christians like to say. There aren't three members. It's not a club.

 It's simple: the Holy Spirit is God Himself
The Holy Spirit is the eternal God.

See, I said, "eternal," so don't call me a *modalist* — a person who thinks Jesus and the Holy Spirit haven't always existed and won't always exist (Hebrews 9:14). To "have the Holy Spirit" means to have God in your heart. But this isn't some vague wishful thinking. God actually takes up residence in your heart, inside your body. You feel His presence. He lives in you *and* He lives in heaven at the same time and anywhere else He wishes. And His being in many places at the same time never changes the fact that there is just one God.

Wait, hold on a second, Bruce

It says right there in John 3:16 that the Father sent the Son into the world, so that's two people, right? No. God Himself had to come and be born as a human so He could die for us. So Jesus was conceived by the Holy Spirit in the womb of a virgin named Mary. You understand that, right? No, of course you don't. In order to explain it to us, God had to use words and ideas that we could understand. So God called Himself "the Father of Jesus" and called Jesus "God's Son."

The Father, Son, and Holy Spirit were all involved in God's coming to earth to save us. But they are not three separate individuals (Matthew 1:20-23; Luke 1:35).

Wasn't God three separate individuals at the baptism of Jesus?

When Jesus came up out of the water after being baptized, the sky opened up, and the Holy Spirit descended from heaven and settled upon Jesus, as a voice from heaven was heard saying, "This is My Son, whom I love, and who pleases Me" (Matthew 3:16-17). Well, do we have three people there?

First, let me ask you some questions. Did Jesus need to be baptized? No. Did Jesus need to be given the Holy Spirit? No, He *is* the Holy Spirit. This event was done by God to show John the Baptist and others present that Jesus was the Savior. What if God didn't do that? How would people know?

John the Baptist said he saw the Spirit descend upon Jesus. That was the sign God the Father told John to look for. God told John that's how he could identify the one who would baptize believers with the Holy Spirit (John 1:32-34).

God does things for a reason. This was a visual illustration — God was teaching something. It doesn't mean God is three people. He's not.

Who gets the Holy Spirit?

God gives His Holy Spirit as a gift to a person when something happens in that person's mind and heart — when they "obey the gospel." It's when they realize they've done God wrong, and turn to Jesus Christ and His sacrifice to be rescued. Jesus gave His life for us, died for us as a sacrifice. The salvation available to us because of the death of Jesus on the cross and resurrection three days later is called the gospel. The word gospel means good news (Romans 10:16).

When a person turns to Jesus Christ for rescue, they are asking God for salvation and they are obeying God — they are "obeying the gospel." God did His part but we also have to do ours. It takes two.

 God says He will give the Holy Spirit to *those who ask Him* (Luke 11:13). And God says He will give the Holy Spirit to *those who obey Him* (Acts 5:32).

God doesn't force anyone
Each of us has to decide to obey the gospel. Romans 1:5 calls that "the obedience of faith." Another way the Bible puts it is we "believe in Jesus." In the most famous verse in the Bible, John 3:16, Jesus said that God loves every single person in this world so much that He gave His only Son to die for us. If any one of us will believe in Jesus, we will not have to pay for our sins by dying the death of the soul, but will instead live with God forever.

> Jesus said that when someone loves and obeys Him, then God the Father and Jesus will come and make their home in that person's heart (John 14:23).

How do I know if a teaching is from the Holy Spirit?

Question: What do these three have in common?
1. You see people in a Christian church acting like they're insane. They tell you their foolish behavior is the result of having God's Holy Spirit. **2.** Members of a certain denomination tell you they know theirs is the one true church because the Holy Spirit tells them it is. But that denomination worships a false Christ and has added to the Word of God. **3.** The elders of another denomination meet to discuss one of the most condemned, most punished sins in the Bible, a sin that is physically and spiritually lethal. They come out of the meeting and announce they've concluded it's not a sin. Why? They say the Holy Spirit told them it's not a sin.
Answer: They don't have God's Holy Spirit — they have a counterfeit.

Now suppose I went around saying, "John Doe is a rapist." And I printed fliers warning about him and asking people to help me spread the word. There's just one problem though — John Doe isn't a rapist. So, how do you think he's going to feel about what I'm doing? Now imagine how God feels when people say His Holy Spirit makes them do evil things.

Who am I to say they have a counterfeit?
No one is at liberty to define the Holy Spirit apart from what we've been told in the Bible. The Bible is our authority. Everything we know about God's Holy Spirit comes from the Bible. That's how you know.

 If someone's calling something the Holy Spirit but it's contrary to the Bible or not found in the Bible, then it is a counterfeit.

We're given the example of the Bereans who searched the Scriptures daily to see if the things the apostle Paul was saying were true, and not contrary to the the Word of God (Acts 17:11).

Is there such as thing as
"a new move of the Holy Spirit"?

Jesus only spoke what God spoke

Jesus said, "I was sent here by My Father (God) and He told Me what to say … The things I say are only those things that I've heard from Him … I don't do anything on My own. I only speak what My Father taught Me" (John 8:26,28; 12:49).

The Holy Spirit only speaks what Jesus spoke

Jesus said, "The Holy Spirit will teach you and will stir up from your memory all the things I've said to you … When the Spirit of truth comes He will lead you into all the truth. He will not speak on His own, but only what He hears from Me. He will honor Me by taking everything I taught you and making it clear in your mind" (John 14:26; 16:13-14).

Jesus was not at liberty to speak something different than what the Father spoke, and the Holy Spirit is not at liberty to speak something different than what Jesus spoke. God is not the author of confusion (1 Corinthians 14:33).

 So if someone tells you the Holy Spirit has something new, it can only mean one thing — *it's not from God.* And if it's not from God, then it's from the devil.

Who speaks on his own?

In John 8:44, Jesus said the devil speaks on his own and is a liar. The devil spoke on his own when he told Eve that God's Word was wrong. He lied and deceived Eve (Genesis 3:4). And whether it's the people who are telling you that the Holy Spirit makes them act like they're insane, or that the Holy Spirit told them to stay in a cult that worships a false Christ and has added to the Word of God, or that the Holy Spirit told them a deadly sin isn't actually a sin — they are all speaking lies because they are speaking on their own. They are not speaking from God's Word (Proverbs 30:6; Revelation 22:18-19).

Is Jesus "not the Holy Spirit"?

"I will come to you"
Jesus was born into a flesh body so He could die on a cross. And after He died and then resurrected from the dead, it was time for Him to go back to heaven. But before Jesus was crucified, He made a promise to all believers. Jesus said, "I will ask My Father and He will send you another Comforter ... I won't leave you as orphans, I will come to you" (John 14:16,18).

 Notice what Jesus said when He told us about the Holy Spirit who will come to believers. Jesus said: *"I* will come to you."

Jesus is "another Comforter"
Jesus is coming to believers now but not in a human body, not in flesh but in Spirit, to continue the work He began while He was in a flesh body. That way Jesus can be with us in a much more intimate, much more effective way — by making His home right in our hearts.

I know, you've probably seen an illustration with the word "Father" at one point of a triangle, "Son" on the second point, "Holy Spirit" on the third, and the words "is not" on the sides and bottom of the triangle. So the claim is that Jesus is not the Holy Spirit and the Father is not Jesus, etc., etc. Poppycock. There they go again, giving people the idea that Christians have three Gods.

One God, not three
Second Corinthians 3:17 says, "The Lord is the Spirit." The "Lord" here is Jesus Christ. In the Book of Revelation, the Holy Spirit takes the apostle John to heaven where he is reunited with Jesus. Jesus makes a long speech, and at one point during the speech we read, "Whoever is willing to hear, listen to what the Spirit is saying." Jesus is talking, and we're told to listen to what the Holy Spirit is

saying (Revelation 2:11). Jesus and the Holy Spirit are one and the same. Romans 8:9 says, "If anyone does not have the Spirit of Christ, then Christ does not recognize them as one of His own."

> "In the beginning was the Word, and the Word was with God, and the Word was God. The Word became flesh and made His dwelling among us" (John 1:1,14). Jesus is the Word of God, and the Bible is the Word of God, the Word of truth (2 Timothy 2:15; Hebrews 4:12).

Jesus called the Holy Spirit "the Spirit of truth" (John 14:16-17). What is truth? Jesus said, "I am the truth" (John 14:6). The truth doesn't change. Hebrews 13:8 says Jesus Christ is the same yesterday, today, and forever. Jesus gives us His Holy Spirit so that we will stay with the truth. The Holy Spirit will keep us in the truth and keep us from error. We have the same truth, the same Word of God, and the same Holy Spirit that the believers had two thousand years ago.

The Spirit = the Word of God
Ephesians 6:17 tells us to "take up and wield the sword of the Spirit — which is the Word of God."

Believers washed by the Spirit = believers washed by the Word
Titus 3:5 says believers are washed by the Holy Spirit. Ephesians 5:26 says believers are washed by the Word.

New birth given by the Holy Spirit = given by the Word of truth
John 3:5 says we are given the new birth by the Holy Spirit, and James 1:18 says we are given the new birth by the Word of truth.

The Holy Spirit lives in us = Christ lives in us
In 1 Corinthians 6:19, the apostle Paul wrote to believers that our bodies are the temple of the Holy Spirit who is in us. In Galatians 2:20, Paul said, "Christ lives in me."

The Holy Spirit = the Spirit of the Son
Galatians 4:6 says that God sends the Spirit of the Son into the hearts of believers.

CREATION	RAISED JESUS
Genesis 1:1 says God created everything	Galatians 1:1 says God the Father raised Jesus from the dead
John 1:3 and Colossians 1:16 say that Jesus created everything	In John 10:17-18, Jesus said He will take back His life after He dies on the cross and is buried
Genesis 1:2 shows that God's Holy Spirit was involved in creation	Romans 8:11 says the Holy Spirit raised Jesus from the dead

INDWELLING SPIRIT	ONE GOD
In John 14:23, Jesus said, "I and My Father will come to them, and We will make our home with them" In John 14:16, Jesus said the Father will send the Holy Spirit In John 16:7, Jesus said He Himself will send the Holy Spirit	In Matthew 16:16-17, Jesus told Peter that it was God the Father who revealed to him that Jesus is the Messiah Jesus is attributing the work of the Holy Spirit (giving understanding about Jesus) to the Father
Second Corinthians 13:5 says Jesus Christ dwells in believers Galatians 4:6 says that God sends the Spirit of the Son into the hearts of believers Philippians 1:19 calls the Holy Spirit the Spirit of Jesus Christ	Isaiah 9:6 says that Jesus is called "the Mighty God" and "the Everlasting Father" The Father, Son, and Holy Spirit are involved in giving spiritual gifts to believers (1 Corinthians 12:11,18,27)
First Corinthians 3:16 says the Holy Spirit dwells in believers In 1 Corinthians 6:19, the apostle Paul wrote to believers that our bodies are the temple of the Holy Spirit who is in us In Galatians 2:20, Paul said "Christ lives in me"	In Acts 5:3, Peter accused Ananias of lying to the Holy Spirit and then in Acts 5:4, referring to the same lie, Peter accused Ananias of lying to God In Romans 8:9, the Holy Spirit is called both the Spirit of God and the Spirit of Christ

Why do I need the Holy Spirit?

We need the Holy Spirit because "without the Holy Spirit no one is able to call Jesus their Lord." And only those who call Jesus their Lord are saved (Romans 10:13; 1 Corinthians 12:3).

Jesus said, "Anyone who has not been given a new spiritual birth by the Holy Spirit — will not be able to enter the kingdom of heaven" (John 3:5). Jesus Christ was conceived in Mary's womb by the power of the Holy Spirit (Luke 1:35). And that same Holy Spirit works in believers to give them a new birth — a new life (Romans 8:11). So you need to have the Holy Spirit because if you don't it means you're doomed, you'll perish forever.

It's God's way of saying, "This belongs to Me"
When God gives you His Holy Spirit, He puts His signature on you. *And God gives you His Holy Spirit as a guarantee to you that you belong to Him.*

Believers are comforted because the presence of God's Holy Spirit inside us makes us know we are going to heaven and will be with God forever. The Holy Spirit is a promise from God — a taste of what's to come. Once God has given you His Holy Spirit, you will have His Holy Spirit forever (John 14:16; Ephesians 1:13-14).

God gave this promise:

> All those whose lives are being led by the Holy Spirit are God's children ... and it is that Holy Spirit in us by whom we can shout to God at the top of our lungs, "Father!" "Father!" The Holy Spirit bears witness together with our new Spirit-birthed life that we are God's children.
>
> - Romans 8:14-16

What will the Holy Spirit do for me?

You can be led to salvation

The Holy Spirit will touch your heart so that you'll feel the pain and remorse of having rejected God and gone your own way (John 16:8). Some will obey the Spirit and turn to Jesus for salvation, but most people will resist the Spirit (Matthew 7:14; 13:10-17; John 3:19; Acts 7:51; 16:14).

You'll know when something's wrong

When you have the Holy Spirit, you're given a new sensitivity to sin — you can feel when something's sinful. You'll have a warning in your heart telling you it's wrong. Yes, everyone has that to some degree — it's called a conscience (Romans 2:15). But it's a whole new level of awareness when you have the Holy Spirit. God will be in your heart helping you. And you'll have a new attitude toward sin — you'll hate it (Psalms 97:10).

 God's Holy Spirit will clean you up and give you a new life
You'll become a new person. You'll gain the ability
to do what's right and avoid doing what's wrong
(2 Corinthians 5:17; 2 Thessalonians 2:13; Titus 3:5).

You'll become more and more like Christ

You will walk in Christ's footsteps by following His example. You'll start to think like Jesus (Romans 8:29; 2 Corinthians 3:17-18; Philippians 2:5).

You will understand the Bible

The Holy Spirit will teach you the deep truths, the mysteries of the Bible, that those who don't have the Holy Spirit can never understand (Isaiah 11:2; 1 Corinthians 2:10; 1 John 2:20,27).

The Holy Spirit can relocate you

God's Holy Spirit will move you to where God wants you to be — to where God has work for you to do. And the Holy Spirit can reveal your calling (Mark 1:12; Acts 8:29; 11:12; 13:1-4; 20:28).

The Holy Spirit will give you strength

You'll have abilities, gifts, talents, and power from the Holy Spirit to do the work God has for you (Acts 1:4,8; 1 Corinthians 2:4-5; Ephesians 3:16).

The Holy Spirit will cry out to God for you

Even when you have the Holy Spirit, you're still human. We all have our weaknesses and handicaps. There are things we should be asking God that we aren't even aware of. So the Holy Spirit helps us by crying out to God for us. The Spirit does this by wailing intensely in ways that can't be put into words. But God hears and understands what the Spirit is saying (Romans 8:26-27).

The Holy Spirit will teach you what to say

If you are arrested because you love Jesus Christ, and you're brought before the tribunals or even before the Antichrist, the devil himself, then the Holy Spirit will teach you what to say (Mark 13:11; Luke 12:12).

Will the Holy Spirit help me fight my addictions?

I want to tell you something

This is for you, if you're struggling with habitual sin. Maybe it's a sexual addiction, or alcoholism, or a drug problem. Maybe you're addicted to anger, covetousness, lust, or an inability to forgive people. The apostle Paul wrote some things that can jolt you, scare you, bring you back into your right mind, and cause you to stop the addiction dead in its tracks. The Holy Spirit has the power to free you from the misery of addiction to sinful habits.

Let me try and explain

I'll tell you what Paul said and give you the references so you can study them yourself. Now this applies only to those who have the Holy Spirit. And yes, even Christians who have the Holy Spirit can and will fall back into habitual sins. That's a reality we have to deal with as long as we're in these bodies made of flesh. The difference is — we struggle and pray to get out of it, and we *do* get free and stand up again (Proverbs 24:16). If you don't have the Holy Spirit, maybe you've been able to fight your addiction in a 12-step program. And there are times when people go there — when they feel hopeless. It can save lives. But you need God's Holy Spirit. Here's why:

 When you have the Holy Spirit you're not alone
First Corinthians 6:17 says that when a person believes in Jesus and becomes united with Him, then the two of them become one Spirit. Your body becomes God's house, the temple of the Holy Spirit. So your body isn't yours anymore — it's not yours to do whatever you want.

Here's the really serious part

Paul explained to us that when you have the Holy Spirit and you engage in sexual immorality, it means God's Holy Spirit is right there in your body with you while you're doing that. And it's the same when you're cursing someone out, or getting drunk, or smoking weed, or fantasizing about sexual sin. When we feel the urge to sin we need to remember that. Then, we'll have a fierce desire to avoid sin and instead use our bodies to glorify God — by obeying God, obeying the Bible (Romans 6:12-13; 1 Corinthians 3:16-17; 6:15-20).

So what will I do?
When you *do* fall into sin, you'll get on your knees and pray to God. You'll beg God to show you a way out of that sin and ask Him to help you take that way out (see 1 Corinthians 10:13). You will always be working and planning to find new ways to live a holy life. (Romans 13:14; Colossians 3:1-10; 1 Peter 1:13-16)

Paul tells us what to do

> My fellow Christians: Let's consider the deep feelings of compassion our merciful God has toward us and has acted on for us. I call upon you therefore to present your bodies to God as a living sacrifice by practicing holiness, which God finds satisfying. It's only logical that you would do this as your duty to God.
> And don't model yourself after the Christ-hating multitudes of this world. But be changed for the better by renewing your mind. Then you will know what God wants. You'll know which are the good things, the ones that come from God, the things that make God feel good — the things that are done by a person who has become an equipped, experienced Christian.
> — Romans 12:1-2

How do we obey Paul's instructions?
We crave the day when Jesus will resurrect us into our permanent, sinless spiritual bodies. But until then, God has equipped us in our lifelong war against sin by putting the Bible in our hands. We obey Paul's instructions by keeping our mind on what is written in the Bible.

David wrote: *Lord, I have treasured up Your Word in my heart because I don't want to sin against You.*

— Psalm 119:11

What does the Holy Spirit expect from me?

I said the Holy Spirit will live inside your body. But there will also be someone else living inside your body. It's the old you — the person you were before God gave you His Holy Spirit (Ephesians 4:22-24). Your job is to fight that old you. The Bible calls that old you "the flesh." Before you had the Holy Spirit, your life was ruled by the flesh.

Romans 8:8 says those who spend their lives serving the flesh are unable to do the things that would bring them God's stamp of approval. But now you can make the Holy Spirit rule your life and subdue the flesh.

> God will freely give more and more of Himself to you.
> He will give you more of His kind favor and His peace — If.
> If what? If you keep gaining more knowledge about God and
> our Lord Jesus Christ. [You find that knowledge in the Bible.]
> God's mighty, miraculous power gives us everything we need
> to live our lives in a godly way.   - 2 Peter 1:2-3

 God gave us precious and magnificent promises
And it's by these promises from God that *we are able to partake of His glorious divine nature*, and make our escape from the sinful lusts of the world that bring destruction.
     - 2 Peter 1:4

When God gives you His Holy Spirit you become a soldier
There will be a war inside you between the flesh and the Spirit. You'll spend the rest of your life fighting the flesh. Galatians 5:17 says:

> Inside of you there is the flesh, the old you, with its immoral desires. There is also the new you, the Spirit-led lover of all things that are right and good. The two of them are enemies.

The things the flesh wants are the opposite of what the Spirit wants. And the things the Spirit wants are the opposite of what the flesh wants.

It's a matter of life and death. Galatians 6:7-8 says:

> Don't be fooled by thinking you can laugh in God's face.
> He won't let you get away with it — He will give you what you deserve.
> Think of it like you're a farmer. There are two types of soil where you can plant your seeds. If the soil you plant in is your flesh — to please your sinful lusts — then you will reap a harvest of death. But if the soil you plant your seeds in is the Holy Spirit living inside you, then the harvest you receive from the Holy Spirit will be eternal life.

Am I saying we're saved by staying away from sinful lusts? No, we're saved by believing in the Lord Jesus Christ. But fighting off sinful lusts is one of the things a saved person does because of the Holy Spirit living in them. It's evidence — proof that the person is truly saved (Luke 6:46-49; Galatians 5:25; James 2:14-26).

Am I saying you'll be perfect?
We are counted as perfect by God when we have the Holy Spirit because then God counts Christ's perfection as though it's ours. But we will never attain to sinless perfection in this life. There are churches who burden their people by teaching them that they can become sinless in this life. But that's a myth, it's not what the Bible teaches, and will only lead to disappointment when you fall into sin. It would be better for us to remember that we are sinners saved by God's grace. We can be reassured that our own experiences as a Christian are normal when we read what the apostle Paul went through, because we see that he agonized with the same struggle against sin as we do:

> I know that in my flesh (the old me) there dwells nothing good.
> Because although there is present within me the willingness to do what is right and good, I come up short.

The fact is, I have the desire to do the good things, but I often find myself not doing them. And the rotten things that I don't want to do — those things I keep on doing.

Because I'm still doing the evil things I don't want to do, I must conclude therefore that it's not me who is doing them. But rather it is the sin that continues to live in me that's doing them.

And after much soul-searching I discovered how this works. Although the two of them are mortal enemies — my desire to do good versus my urges to do evil — the two of them are living together, sharing quarters in my body.

Look, the new me, the Spirit-led Paul, jumps for joy at the thought of doing right by obeying God's way.

But there's another force present within me that wages war against my rational mind. It overpowers those feelings of joy, catches me in its trap, and I'm stuck in sin again.

I'm so tired of this — it's like being punched over and over. Who will deliver me from this body that suffers through sin and death?

- Romans 7:18-24

Paul was speaking rhetorically when he said, "Who will deliver me?" He knew who would deliver him from sin and death. It's the Lord Jesus Christ. Paul suffered like we do (Acts 14:15).

But we fight on. In Romans 8:23, Paul writes about the turmoil that goes on inside a believer. We shed tears over our sin. We groan in the deepest part of our being. We're angry, frustrated. We look forward to — welcome — the day when Jesus will deliver us from these flesh bodies and give us eternal, sinless, spiritual bodies. (1 Corinthians 15:50-58)

How do I fight the flesh with the Spirit?

> Just as with any army, when we're enlisted into God's army
> He makes available the weapons we need to be successful.

We can have the ability to fight off the fiery darts of temptation that the devil throws at us and strive to live a holy life by taking on God's strength and power. The apostle Paul tells us how to do that. In Ephesians 6:10-18, Paul lays out the armor of God for us. And the weapon we use on the offensive, when we are in close hand-to-hand combat with sin, is "the sword of the Spirit, which is the Word of God" (Ephesians 6:17). Jesus taught us how to use the Word of God as a weapon against the devil's temptations (Matthew 4:1-11).

Fight the flesh by walking in the Spirit
And we're commanded to fight the flesh by doing what the Bible calls "walking by the Spirit." Galatians 5:16 says:

> If you walk (live your life) by the guiding light of the Holy Spirit in you, then there's no way you would want to indulge yourself trying to find pleasure in your old sinful addictions (the flesh).

How do I walk in the Spirit? Romans 13:14 says:

> Clothe yourself with the Lord Jesus Christ, and do not spend your time planning how to try and gratify the burning lusts of your flesh.

 James has encouraging words:
Place yourself in submission to God and obey Him.
Strongly resist the devil — hold your ground, refuse to be moved — and the devil will flee from you.

- James 4:7

How are people being deceived about the Holy Spirit?

There are false teachings about how a person receives the Holy Spirit. I must warn you to beware of people who are misleading millions around the world with a harmful and divisive deception.

Question: Have you believed in Jesus Christ and been saved?
Yes? Great. That means you have received the Holy Spirit. You're good to go. But not according to some denominations. They say you're inferior to them — that you don't have the full relationship with Jesus Christ and power from the Holy Spirit that they have.

What do they claim has put them in this more advanced state?
In their own words, it's this: *"Baptism with the Holy Spirit, with the evidence of speaking in tongues."* This, they allege, is the second stage you need in order to become a complete, effective Christian.

They are in error because:

1. A person is *baptized* with the Holy Spirit when they *receive* the indwelling Holy Spirit.
2. "Speaking in tongues" is not "the evidence" that a person has the Holy Spirit.

Do they teach error because they've misunderstood what the Bible says? There is that. But there's more to it. This is another one of the devil's devices to steal the Bible away from God's children.

I'd like you to see this. You can go online and look at what they're doing to people with this false teaching of being *"baptized in the Holy Spirit with the evidence of speaking in tongues."* What you see is people acting like lunatics. They're shaking, trembling, and uttering ungodly noises from their mouths. Those noises aren't words — they don't make sense, they don't teach anyone the Bible, they don't do anybody any good.

How did seeing that make you feel? If I was somewhere and people started acting like that, I would get myself out of there fast.

That's all the evidence we need

If that babbling is what they call "speaking in tongues" then we can dismiss this whole thing just based on that. God doesn't deal in insanity.

 God is not a God of disorder. He is a God of peace in church. God wants everything done in an orderly and respectable manner.   - 1 Corinthians 14:33,40

When you watched them, did you hear them talking about the wonderful works of God? No? Neither did I. The Bible says that when the disciples spoke in tongues, they spoke about the wonderful works of God, and everyone in the crowd understood what they said (Acts 2:1-11). This proves that what we see online is a fraud.

They're misleading God's children

And by God's children, I mean adults — whether believers or nonbelievers. They're misleading nonbelievers by making them think that Christianity is insanity. Nonbelievers are God's children too. God created them, loves them, and wants them to come to Him. But when they encounter this false teaching, they will either reject Christianity, concluding that it's madness or, even worse, they will think it *is* Christianity, join these lunatics, and help them lead more people astray.

As you can see online, they're doing this to actual children too — minors. It's spiritual child abuse. And they call it "God's Holy Spirit." I can't even imagine how angry God must be.

You really need to understand how serious this is

When you watch them doing that foolishness, you know what you don't see? You don't see them doing what they *should* be doing. You don't see them with their Bibles open, sharing God's Word with each other.

The devil has stolen God's Word from them by replacing the Word of God with a counterfeit Holy Spirit.

The Holy Spirit isn't going to give us anything the Bible hasn't given us. Do you know what to do if someone tells you the Holy Spirit's new thing is for you to hop on one foot? You ask them to show you where it says that in the Bible. And when someone tells you to utter babbling noises, ask them to show you in the Bible where Jesus and the apostles did that. They can't show you, because Jesus and the apostles never did that and neither should you. Jesus and the apostles spoke words in sentences, full of meaning. And we are to do the same, to teach people the Word of God using understandable words that their minds can absorb and use. We must never follow the bad example of those who act foolishly and call it the Holy Spirit (Acts 17:11; 1 John 4:1).

Where does this false teaching come from?

The whole false teaching of believers needing to be "subsequently baptized with the Holy Spirit with the evidence of speaking in tongues" comes from a misunderstanding of the one-time-only, special occurences arranged by God through the Holy Spirit in Acts chapters 2, 8, 10, and 19. All of those occurences were for a specific purpose: to show that everyone was equal in God's eyes when it comes to being saved and receiving God's Holy Spirit. Each one highlighted that no group of believers was considered less worthy of God's grace than another group.

They're putting something where it doesn't belong

It's wrong for people to say that believers today should have the same experience as certain believers did in the Book of Acts. Those who try to have the same experience are like people who reenact historical events. Except that *these* reenactors are doing grave spiritual harm. They're relegating millions of good Christians to second class status. And that's just what God said not to do — in the very same Bible passages these deceivers misuse to teach their false Holy Spirit baptism theory.

What's the harm in false teachings about the Holy Spirit?

In 1 Corinthians 12:27-31, Paul said not all believers speak in tongues. Paul listed tongues as one of the gifts of the Holy Spirit, along with the gifts of healing, teaching, leadership, and helping others.

 Paul did not set the gift of tongues apart as the one gift that must be present in a believer to prove they've been baptized with the Holy Spirit.

People are being taught to manufacture babbling noises

It's absurd to claim a believer must speak in tongues as proof that they've been baptized with the Holy Spirit. There's no basis in the Bible to make that claim. And you know what's happening because of that false teaching? People are forcing themselves into some sort of trance-like state and uttering nonsense, in desperate attempts to get themselves into the so-called elite group of those who have the gift of tongues. Children are doing this — mumbling and babbling. Is it follow-the-leader? hypnosis? demonic possession? or are they just faking? Whatever the reason why they are acting like lunatics, it has nothing to do with God. God is not making them shake, tremble, and produce unintelligible sounds.

The results don't prove the theory

I observe the pastors who teach that theory — that believers must be subsequently baptized with the Holy Spirit with the evidence of speaking in tongues. They say it gives them a complete relationship with Christ and power from the Holy Spirit. Really? Where's the evidence? I don't see it. I see a lot of huffing and puffing, showmanship, smoke and mirrors.

But they do teach the Bible sometimes

Yes, of course they teach the Bible. And they might teach much that's correct. But the Bible isn't their primary focus. They seem to be trying to separate the Holy Spirit from the Bible. They seem to be putting the Holy Spirit above the Bible in importance. From what I've seen, only a small percentage of what the "two-stage" pastors do in worship services is Bible teaching.

I've known and watched serious Bible teachers who *don't* accept the two-stage baptism theory. They are gifted, learned teachers, and they teach the Word of God diligently, line by line. They make familiarity with the Bible the central part of their worship services. I'll take them any day over the supposedly more complete "two-stage baptism" teachers.

There's a trick the devil uses
The most effective way to convince someone to accept error, such as this false teaching of a two-stage baptism of the Holy Spirit, is to bring error in alongside truth. Because of the presence of what people know is truth, they will be more willing to accept the error even if they have doubts about it and suspect it might be false. Why else would millions around the world join this denomination, which teaches something so obviously unbiblical and un-Christlike, and which looks so demonic?

Were the disciples "drunk in the Spirit"?

The Bible doesn't say the disciples acted like they were drunk on the day they received the Holy Spirit — because they didn't. The Bible says that *some of the skeptics in the crowd* said the disciples were drunk. But look at *why* they said that. Acts 2:13 tells us they said it to mock the disciples. They were mad that common people were preaching. They thought: *These people weren't ordained by the local church, who do they think they are?* They did the same thing to Jesus (John 7:15). Sometimes, people who disagree with something are too intellectually lazy to come up with an argument and decide instead to insult the person they disagree with. The disciples were not drunk, and they weren't acting drunk (Acts 2:15).

I had someone at the Quiz try and slip one by me. He told me the Bible says, "Don't be drunk with wine but be drunk with the Spirit." But he changed a word. The Bible says, "Don't be drunk with wine but be *filled* with the Spirit" (Ephesians 5:18).

 The Bible says drunkenness is a serious sin
The Holy Spirit would never contradict the Bible.
The Holy Spirit would never call evil good by using drunkenness as an illustration of spiritual gifts
(Galatians 5:21).

Yes, there may be some similarities between wine and the Holy Spirit. The Holy Spirit gives joy to a believer. And the Bible says wine makes people's hearts cheerful. But there's a big difference between drinking wine in moderation and getting drunk. The Holy Spirit won't imitate a sin (Psalm 104:15; Ecclesiastes 9:7; Galatians 5:22).

There is a blasphemous false teaching called "being drunk in the Spirit" where people stagger and fall, and claim it's because of the influence of the Holy Spirit. Imitating a sin and claiming the Holy Spirit did it is an offense against the Holy Spirit. Don't do that — it's a work of the devil.

Does the Holy Spirit create two classes of Christians?

The Holy Spirit doesn't divide believers into two groups. The Holy Spirit unites believers. We are one household of believers, one body. One Spirit, not two. God doesn't have pet Christians.

Ephesians 2:18-19 says that because we go through Jesus Christ, every believer has direct access to God by one Spirit. And because we have the same Spirit, every one of us has equal citizenship in God's kingdom — we are all members of the one family.

First Corinthians 12:13 says that all believers are baptized by one Spirit into one body, and all believers drink from one Spirit. In Ephesians 4:1-6 the apostle Paul wrote this to all believers:

> I insist that you live your lives in a way that your behavior conforms to the high calling to which you've been called. Never prideful, but always treating fellow Christians with tenderness, with a gentle strength that's not easily irritated. Sticking together with the true, unfeigned love that God has put in our hearts. Work diligently to keep the peaceful unity that all of you have from the Holy Spirit.

 There is one body of believers and one Spirit ...
one Lord, one faith, one baptism. There is one God,
who is above all, and is the Father of all of you.
He works through all of you and is within all of you.

One body
In I Corinthians 12:4-7, the apostle Paul taught us that no Christian is inferior to any other Christian. So having a gift, whether it be speaking in tongues or any other, doesn't put you into a special class of Christian. There are no first-class Christians and no second-class Christians. Paul said that no Christian is lacking because we are all part of the same body, and that body is Christ's body (Romans 12:5).

In Colossians 2:9-10, Paul wrote that Christians are complete because we have Christ in whom is the sum total of God in a human body.

In Acts 2:38-40, people who heard the apostle Peter preach the gospel and were "pierced to the heart" asked Peter what they should do. Peter told them to repent, believe in Jesus Christ, and they would receive the gift of the Holy Spirit. We're told that three thousand people did just that, and they were added to the believers. That's all they did and all they needed to do. They were completely Christian, no lack. *Peter didn't tell them they were incomplete.* They *were* complete. A believer is born of the Spirit and baptized with the Spirit when they believe in Jesus Christ as their Lord and Savior. It's not two separate things but one (Galatians 3:26-27).

United as one
On the night before He would be crucified, Jesus prayed fervently for His disciples, asking God to bless them. And four times during that prayer Jesus asked the Father the same thing: that those who believe in Him be united as one (John 17:11,21,22,23).

Treat others as better than us, not lower than us
Christians aren't supposed to be ambitious for self-promotion, creating cliques and rivalries. We don't display feelings of pride against our brothers and sisters, but rather we're to be humble. We are to love our fellow Christians kindly and affectionately, and respect them in a way that makes them feel they are more valuable than us. We're to clothe ourselves with humility and treat our fellow Christians as though they outrank us. We can only do that because God's Holy Spirit is present in us and among us (Romans 12:10; Ephesians 4:3; Philippians 2:3; 1 Peter 5:5).

The *whole* false two-stage Holy Spirit baptism teaching is self-exalting to the core ... "we're better Christians than you because we've been baptized by the Holy Spirit, and we speak in tongues but you don't." The Holy Spirit unites us with love. Satan is prideful and divides.

How do I know if I have the Holy Spirit?

Jesus said:
"I tell you a solemn truth — no one can go to heaven who has not been *given a new birth* by the Holy Spirit." - John 3:5

John the Baptist said he baptized in water but Jesus will *baptize* with the Holy Spirit (Luke 3:16). And in Acts 1:5, Jesus said that John baptized with water but those who believe in Him will be baptized with the Holy Spirit.

Being given a new birth by the Holy Spirit and being baptized with the Holy Spirit are one and the same thing. But how do you know if it's happened to you?

The fruit of the Spirit

The evidence that you have the Holy Spirit is not in physical manifestations but in what the Bible calls the fruit of the Spirit. Jesus compared people to trees (Matthew 7:16-20). The fruit of the Spirit is the good fruit, which the Holy Spirit produces in believers. So by fruit we mean the results, the changes, the new characteristics which the believer has because of God's Holy Spirit living inside them. The Bible tells us there are nine of them. The fruit that the Holy Spirit produces in a person is:

1) the ability to truly love others
2) an inner feeling of joy
3) the ability to be at peace
4) the ability to not behave bitterly toward others
5) a concern for the well-being of others
6) a zealous love of that which is good
7) an unshakable trust in God that makes them into
    someone others feel they can trust
8) a gentle strength
9) the ability to resist the lusts of the flesh   (Galatians 5:22-23)

You'll know you have the Holy Spirit when you become a new creation (2 Corinthians 5:17).

The apostle Paul instructs us:

> Those who belong to Christ have crucified the flesh with its cravings and impulses. We've been given life by the Spirit, so we should conduct our lives in step with the Spirit. And we must shun self-love, those inclinations towards bigheaded delusions of grandeur.
>
>   - Galatians 5:24-26

Can I do this?
Yes. The apostle Paul wrote:

I can do all things through Christ who gives me strength.

           - Philippians 4:13

Chapter Seven

Being
a Christian

Don't just listen to the Word of God — do what it says.
Otherwise, you're only fooling yourself.

- James 1:22

We follow Christ ... that's what Christians do. Christ showed us what to do by His example and by His teachings. Christians are to imitate Christ and become more and more like Him.

What's it going to cost me to believe in Jesus?

When Jesus encountered people for the first time, He wasn't thinking, *I'd better be nice to them or they won't join My church.* Jesus didn't think, *I'll just love them first and tell them about the serious stuff later.* Jesus knew they would feel deceived later on when they learned that following Him brings trouble. They would turn and run from the spiritual warfare, and leave the work unfinished. Jesus was honest with strangers. He told them right up front what it would cost them to follow Him — He didn't use bait and switch.

When Jesus knew that someone who came to Him wasn't sincere, He would discourage them from following Him. Jesus doesn't want halfhearted people mixed in with His genuine followers, disheartening them or enticing them to sin and disobedience. Jesus wants holiness in His church.

There are many Christians who say the right things and do lots of things that look good, but when they meet Jesus He will say to them:

> "I never knew you: depart from Me,
> you who work iniquity."   - Matthew 7:23

What did they do wrong? They never let themselves be influenced, shaped, and changed by the words of Jesus, because they were *too busy* to study their Bibles. So when Jesus says to them, "I never knew you," what He means is, "You never made the effort to get to know Me" (Deuteronomy 4:29; Hosea 4:6; 2 Timothy 3:15).

And what is this "work iniquity"? It means that as far as breaking God's law goes, their attitude was, "That's the way it's done around here." Jesus won't accept them because they didn't care about obeying Him (1 Samuel 15:22-23; Jeremiah 6:16; Luke 6:46-49).

"Working iniquity" includes those in denominations who mislead God's children with false teachings and "the commandments of men." It means they never truly followed Jesus. They don't have the Holy Spirit — they have a deceiving spirit (Mark 7:6-9, 13; Luke 9:23; Acts 5:32; Romans 6:6; Philippians 2:5; 1 Timothy 4:1).

What was it then that Jesus had, and His true followers have, but the others, these so-called Christians, are lacking? OBEDIENCE and LOVE — a Christian *must* have both. The Pharisees thought they had obedience, but they lacked love. And there are many Christians in this day and age who think they have love, but they lack obedience (see 2 John 1:6).

Someone might say, "Hold on now, I think *you're* wrong! I too know a little bit about how this works, and I know that all you have to do is believe; believe in Jesus and you're in, you're going to heaven." And I say, "Yes!" When the Philippian jailer asked Paul and Silas what he must do to be saved, they replied, "Believe on the Lord Jesus Christ and you will be saved" (Acts 16:30-31).

But believing is just the beginning. Many churches make their people think you just say the words "I believe," and then ease into a nice hot bath of grace. That's nothing more than lip service — and God hates it. That mind-set is a slippery slope, whose end result is a congregation which has been made to believe that a desire to obey God is offensive to God. They say things like "sin is sin: no sin is worse than any other" (Isaiah 29:13-15; 65:4).

Jesus didn't need to be saved — He is God Himself — but Jesus performed the greatest act of love *and* obedience by living a sinless life as a man, and then laying down His life, going to the cross. Jesus did that in order to make salvation available for every one of us — and to teach us by His example (John 14:31; Hebrews 5:8; 1 Peter 2:21).

Can you name the three things that are necessary for you to be saved? They are: 1) God's grace
                            2) Your faith (believing)
                            3) Your works (obedience)

Now you might ask me, "Where are you getting this? I've never heard this in my church." And I would ask you — who do you listen to, your church or the Word of God? Please study James 2:14-26; 1 John 2:3-7; 2 Timothy 2:19; Hebrews 12:14; and Matthew 7:13-14.

Yes, Jesus did all the earning of our salvation — that's God's grace. But Jesus warned us that genuine faith is costly; if we want to follow Him, we must pay dearly. When we say "I believe," we're making a solemn promise to give everything, even if it means being killed in the line of duty (Luke 10:27; 14:25-35; Romans 5:15; Ephesians 2:8-9; 6:10-18; Jude 1:3-4).

 If your faith in God doesn't move you to work for God, then your faith is as useless as a dead person's body.

- James 2:26

Jesus doesn't want you to believe in Him in a way that won't save you. Jesus doesn't want you:

— if you're not willing to make Him your #1 (Luke 9:59-62)
— if your faith in Him is superficial (John 2:23-25)
— if you're just following Him for the fish sandwiches (John 6:24-27)
— if you're not willing to obey Him:

> "Not everyone who says to Me, 'Lord, Lord,' shall enter
> into the kingdom of heaven; but the one who does the will
> of My Father who is in heaven [shall enter into the kingdom
> of heaven.]"
>
> - Jesus, Matthew 7:21

Obedience or lack of obedience — that's how Jesus can tell who loves Him and who doesn't. It's how He decides who He wants to be friends with (John 14:21-24; 15:14).

> "My mother and My brethren are the people who hear
> the Word of God and do it."
>
> - Jesus, Luke 8:21

Jesus can't stand phonies. If you're thinking of joining His little flock but you don't plan on obeying Him — stay home. Go to Acts 5:1-13 and read what Jesus did to two pretenders who joined His church. Don't mess with Jesus.

So, why the big deal about obedience? Well, do you know what sin is? It's disobedience. That's right. The definition of sin is — the breaking of God's law (1 John 3:4).

Sin is what caused all the trouble in the first place. And our sin, our disobedience, is what Jesus paid the price for. It's the reason He gave Himself over to those fierce Roman soldiers who whipped Him, mocked Him, punched Him, spit in His face, and hammered nails through His hands and feet, pinning Him to a wooden cross to die (Matthew 26:66-68; 27:26-31; Mark 14:65; Romans 5:12; 6:23).

But Christians sin. Yes, we mess up, sometimes horribly.
And God says:

> If we confess our sins,
> He is faithful and just to forgive us our sins,
> and to cleanse us from all unrighteousness.
>
> - 1 John 1:9 (KJV)

That's the great thing about Christianity.

Do I only have two choices: repent or die?

A young man was looking over my pamphlet display in Harvard Square. He was okay until he saw the title "Repent or Die." He didn't like the fact that there wasn't a third option.

The very first thing Jesus told us to do is:

"Repent."   - Matthew 4:17

To repent means to change your mind about the direction in which your life is going. Everyone needs to repent (Luke 13:3; Romans 3:23; 6:23).

In Luke 19:1-10 there's a wonderful story of repentance. A man named Zacchaeus lived in the city of Jericho. He had been busy making himself rich by stealing at his job as a big shot tax collector. Then Zacchaeus heard that Jesus had come to his neighborhood. He tried to see Jesus, but there were too many people crowding around Jesus, and Zacchaeus wasn't a tall man. So he ran ahead on the path and climbed up a tree so he could see Jesus when He came that way. Jesus saw him in the tree, and said, "Zacchaeus, climb down, let's go to your house."

Zacchaeus climbed down, and he was so excited he was jumping for joy as he and Jesus walked to his house. The people were mad though. They said, "Why is Jesus going to that sinner's house?"

But at his house, Zacchaeus stood up, and told Jesus that he wanted to pay back the money he stole, and do good things from now on. He repented. And Jesus said, "Salvation has come to this house today."

Zacchaeus showed himself to be one of the family of faith. The Son of Man had indeed come to seek and save those who had become lost.

Jesus doesn't want our spiritual body to die in hell. That's what really matters. If we don't repent, then our sinfulness, our disobedience of God's laws, will lead to the death of our soul — a spiritual death (Matthew 5:29-30; 10:28; John 3:16).

When we hear that some especially evil person died a violent death, we might think they got what they deserved. The problem with thinking that way is it makes us feel good about ourselves. Jesus said:

> "When you hear that people died violently, don't sit back and think they must have been the world's worst sinners and therefore they're doomed but you're all set. Maybe they are doomed. But I'm telling you — unless you repent of your sins, you too will be doomed to die the second death forever."
>
> - Luke 13:4-5

Jesus seized upon our faulty thinking as an opportunity to warn us, and to get us to think seriously about what really matters. God wants us to acknowledge that our heart and mind are contaminated with twisted, perverse, and sinful feelings and desires. God wants us to feel sorry about our sinfulness. He wants us to have a strong, sincere desire to have something done about it (Psalm 51:17; Mark 7:20-23; Luke 15:11-24; 2 Corinthians 7:10).

God wants us to realize that Jesus Christ is the only one who can save us from our sinfulness, and who can save us from God's anger, and from hell. Why? Because Jesus died in our place (Romans 5:6-11).

But God requires action on our part. We must get up and go to Jesus Christ. God wants the kind of repentance Zacchaeus showed, that drives a person to Christ, seeking forgiveness. That's the repentance that leads to salvation and eternal life (Matthew 11:27-30).

And when we repent and go to Christ, He will give us the desires of our heart. He will forgive us for our sins, and wash us clean. Jesus will comfort us, dry our tears, give us a new heart, and a new life (2 Corinthians 5:17-21; Revelation 21:4).

Will God forgive me if I ask Him to?

You might be disqualified or get fired in this world because of an indiscretion. But it's not that way with Jesus. You confess your sin, tell Him you're sorry, and He accepts you 100% as if it never happened. It's like when a child does something wrong, and they go to their parent and say they're sorry. The parent hugs them and kisses them.

Everybody sins every day. But the Bible says there are wicked people, and there are righteous people. *If everybody sins every day, then why are some wicked and some righteous?* I want to show you a verse:

> Things won't go well for those who cover up their sins and hide them. But God will have compassion if they confess their sins and turn away from them.   - Proverbs 28:13

1) What is confession? Confession is being honest with God.

God gave Adam and Eve one instruction in the Garden — stay away from the tree that teaches you how to take pleasure from God's creation in an evil way. But the Evil One charmed Eve and got her to eat from that tree, and she got Adam to eat.
Then God asked Adam and Eve, "Did you eat from the tree that I told you to stay away from?"
Adam replied, "Yes, I did eat, but the woman You gave me got me to do it — she gave it to me."
And Eve replied, "Yes, I did eat, but the Evil One tricked me" (Genesis 2:17; 3:1-13).

Adam and Eve had two sons, Cain and Abel. And one day, in a fit of jealous rage, Cain murdered Abel.
God asked Cain, "Where is your brother?"
Cain replied, "I don't know" (Genesis 4:8-9).
Adam blamed Eve and Eve blamed the Evil One, but they were honest with God — they confessed. And Cain? He's a liar.

How did lying to God work out for Cain? How is Cain remembered? First John 3:12 says Cain is a child of the Evil One — the devil.

Eve sinned. But later, in Genesis 3:20, we read that Eve is "the mother of all living." Through Eve would come Jesus Christ, by whom a person can live forever.

2) Can you confess anything? Yes, anything. God already knows about it anyway. Be honest, and sincere.

David, king of Israel, seduced a man's wife and she became pregnant. The man was one of David's soldiers, named Uriah. David sent for Uriah from the battlefield and told him to take some time off to be with his wife. That way Uriah would think the child was his. But Uriah loved king David so much, that instead of going to be with his wife he spent the night outside David's door to protect David. Before Uriah went back to the fighting, David handed him a letter and told him to give it to Joab, Uriah's commander. In the letter, David told Joab to take his men to the front lines. Then, without telling Uriah, they were to withdraw. Uriah was left alone, and he died in battle.

One of my favorite passages in the Bible tells us the way God caused David to come to his senses and confess his sins. You can read about it in 2 Samuel 12:1-13. And yes, God forgave David.

3) How many times can you confess? An unlimited number of times.

> A righteous person falls seven times and rises again,
> But a wicked person will fall into evil.   - Proverbs 24:16
> > *The number "seven" is used here to mean an unlimited number*

 Don't be afraid — God loves to forgive
Psalms 86:5 says:

> Oh Lord, You are so nice, so willing to forgive.
> You pour out Your kindness to everyone who
> calls out to You.

What is the unforgivable sin?

Don't worry, committing the unforgivable sin is not a simplistic or superstitious thing. It's not like uttering a magical sentence that once you've spoken you can't take back, your fate is sealed, and you're doomed forever with no hope. If you're worried that you've committed the unforgivable sin — relax, you haven't.

How did this come up?
On several occasions Jesus healed people by driving evil spirits out of them. Many who saw the miracles were amazed. But certain religious leaders called scribes and Pharisees became jealous of Jesus and they hated Him (Mark 11:18; Luke 4:33-37; 8:24-39; 9:38-45).

What did they do?
The scribes and Pharisees wanted to get the people to stop following Jesus, so they said that Jesus was possessed by the devil. And they told the people it was the devil who gave Jesus the ability to drive out evil spirits. I don't know if they realized it, but they went too far. They crossed a line (Mark 3:22; John 11:47-48).

How did Jesus respond?
Jesus let them have it. He said:

> "People may be forgiven for every sin and blasphemy:
> but blasphemy against the Holy Spirit will not be forgiven.
> If anyone says a word against the Son of Man, they may
> be forgiven: but if anyone speaks against the Holy Spirit,
> they will not be forgiven, not in this world or the one to come."

> - Matthew 12:31-32

A person commits blasphemy when they speak slanderous insults against another, and it's especially bad when done against God.

Mark 3:30 tells us that the scribes and Pharisees committed blasphemy against the Holy Spirit when they said that Jesus was possessed by the devil and that He drove out evil spirits by the power of the devil. In Matthew 12:28, Jesus said He drove out evil spirits by the power of God's Holy Spirit. So the scribes and Pharisees were saying that God's Holy Spirit was the devil.

Jesus was speaking as a man, not as God

Notice that Jesus didn't say *He* drove out evil spirits. Jesus said He drove out evil spirits by the power of the Holy Spirit. Jesus was speaking as a man when He warned people not to blaspheme the Holy Spirit. That's why He referred to Himself as the Son of Man, and said a person may be forgiven if they blaspheme Him — the man. It was Jesus *the man* who told the scribes and Pharisees they would never be forgiven — He was saying, "Look, don't say the Holy Spirit is the devil. God's Holy Spirit is your only chance, so don't reject the Holy Spirit."

The Holy Spirit is the one who touches a person's heart to make them feel sorrow for their sins. It's only by the work of the Holy Spirit that a person is going to be led to the truth, to repentance, and to Christ for forgiveness (Mark 1:10-12; Luke 1:38; 4:14; John 15:26; 16:7-8; Philippians 2:5-7).

 It isn't simply that the scribes and Pharisees spoke slanderous insults against the Holy Spirit. *Rejecting the Holy Spirit was the unforgivable sin because they were rejecting the only way they could be forgiven for their sin — the drawing by the Holy Spirit to the Savior, Jesus Christ.*

If you're a Christian, you haven't committed the unforgivable sin. But to ease your mind, ask God to forgive you.
You mean God will forgive the unforgivable sin? Of course He will. He would have forgiven the scribes and Pharisees if they had changed their minds and let the Holy Spirit draw them to Christ. If you're not a Christian and worried, then go to Christ and find peace of mind (Matthew 11:29).

What does it mean to be "born again"?

One day I was doing the Bible Quiz ministry in an area of Boston called Downtown Crossing, and Karlos came by to spend time with me. Karlos is one of my favorite Christians. Two young women came up to take the Quiz at the same time that another couple also came up. So I talked to the couple and Karlos talked to the two young women. They were behind me and I overheard the first thing Karlos said to them: "Are you born again?" I was struck by that. Wow, he got it, right to the heart of the matter, what a great opening question. I knew then that I had to write something about what it means to be born again.

Will God let you into heaven because you obeyed man-made rules, or because you've satisfied the requirements of your church? What if you have a degree from the best Bible college, been put into a position of leadership, or you're a respected teacher?

There was a man named Nicodemus who achieved all the requirements listed above. He lacked nothing, he had the credentials. He might have been thinking that God will move him to the front of the line when he goes to heaven.

And there was a new teacher in town. His name was Jesus. Nicodemus had been watching Jesus, and one night he decided to pay Him a visit. Maybe it was professional courtesy, or maybe Nicodemus wanted to pat Jesus on the back and give Him some encouragement. Nicodemus might have been thinking he'd flatter Jesus a little, have a nice chat, and then go back to his comfortable life (John 3:1-10).

Nicodemus said to Jesus:

> "Oh great one, we all know that you're a teacher who has been sent by God because no one could perform the miracles you do if God wasn't with them."
>
> - John 3:2

But Jesus wasn't into small talk, and He wasn't into making people feel comfortable with their lives. Jesus didn't say, "Thanks for the compliment." He didn't tell Nicodemus to use this right-now-moment to plant his best financial seed into Jesus' ministry. Jesus acted like He didn't hear a word Nicodemus said. It was as though Jesus knew Nicodemus was coming, had been waiting for him, and had prepared what He would say to him.

Jesus said, "If you're not born again, then you can't go to heaven."

Boom! What? Born again? Can't go to heaven? What *was* Jesus talking about? Nicodemus was confused, he never expected *that*. But Jesus explained it to him, and I think Nicodemus got it (John 19:38-40).

 When someone belongs to Christ, they become a new person: it's out with the old, and in with the new.

- 2 Corinthians 5:17

Being born again is not something you can earn. It's not something your church can give you. God's not impressed because you're a big man in a big church. The apostle Paul had all the credentials, but after he was born again he said the credentials he once relied on were as useless as garbage (Philippians 3:1-11).

Being born again is something only God can give you. But you must have the right heart. What is the right heart? It has to do with how you respond when you hear the truth from the Bible (Luke 11:39; Galatians 6:15; study the parable of the sower in Matthew 13:18-23).

You can read about some who were born again in Luke 19:1-10; Luke 18:9-14; and Luke 7:36-50; see 1 Peter 1:23. When you're born again God gives you His Holy Spirit to comfort you and help you live a brand new life for Him (Ezekiel 36:25-27; Romans 8:11).

The change is so radical, it's called being born again

Do I need to be baptized to be saved?

Being dipped in water by the "right" denomination is not what
saves you. Jesus saves you. Baptism is between you and Jesus.

Has someone told you that you must be baptized to be saved?
Then you've met someone who's in a cult.

How is a person saved?
Jesus Himself told us in some of the most well known words in the
Bible, words we've heard so many times that maybe we don't
appreciate what Jesus is telling us:

> God loves all the people of the world so much, that He
> sacrificed His only Son, Jesus Christ, so that whoever believes
> in Jesus will not perish but will have everlasting life. - John 3:16

God's Holy Spirit worked through the apostle Paul to explain
salvation. In Ephesians 2:8, Paul told us that we're saved by the
grace of God. Salvation is a free gift which God gives us. There's
only one way we can receive this free gift, and that is through our
faith, by believing in what Jesus did for us. Jesus gave Himself as the
sinless sacrifice. Jesus shed His blood, died on a cross to pay for our
sins, and rose from death victoriously (1 Corinthians 15:1-4; Titus 3:4-7).

It means that instead of facing the wrath of God to receive the
punishment we deserve for our sins, we can claim the punishment
that innocent Jesus received as though it is ours. Then we can enjoy a
full relationship with God, eternally. That's amazing.

And those who believe in Jesus are sealed with a mark of the genuine-
ness of their faith, called the baptism of the Holy Spirit. What does
that mean? Jesus told us in John 14:23, where He said that if anyone
loves Him and shows that love by zealously guarding His words,

then God the Father and Jesus will love that person. And they will come and make their home in that person's heart — they will live there. That is the baptism of the Holy Spirit.

The cults have an evil plan

When they say you can't be saved unless you're baptized first, what they really mean is "you can't be saved unless you're baptized into our denomination." They indoctrinate their recruits into a salvation-by-works mindset. Once baptized, the recruit feels pressured into a lifetime of working for the cult, hoping that by pleasing the cult they might eventually earn their salvation.

So, what's the point of water baptism?

Let me answer that by asking *you* a question:

Are works necessary to salvation?

Here's my answer: "Yes." Why do I say yes?

Because in his epistle, James wrote, "Faith without works is dead." In fact, he wrote it three times. In James 2:17, 20, and 26 (KJV).

It is absolutely critical though, that you know *when* works are to be done, and it is definitely *not before* you are saved. For anyone to say you can't be saved before you are water baptized is — rude! Why? Because salvation is God's free gift, and do you want to take from God His right, His ability, to give you a gift? Do you think He needs your little act of being immersed in water? As though the sacrifice of Jesus on the cross wasn't enough to save you? It's like spitting on God's gracious gift; it's an insult, a slap in the face to Jesus (Ezekiel 36:25-27).

Water baptism has zero value in the earning of our salvation — Jesus did all the earning.

 Water baptism is only for those who are *already* saved
It's an act of obedience done by those who have been regenerated by God's Holy Spirit. Water baptism is only a symbol of the reality, it's not the reality. The reality is the believer's baptism with the Holy Spirit, which starts a Christian on a new life (Acts 10:47-48; Romans 6:3-5; 1 Peter 3:21).

Does it matter if I'm baptized in Jesus' name or in the name of the Father, Son, and Holy Spirit?

One day while I was setting up my display to do the Quiz, I noticed a woman standing near me. I should have said hello to her. I didn't realize she was waiting patiently for me to finish setting up. When I was done she came closer to ask me a question. She was a Christian and she wanted to know if a person should be baptized "in Jesus' name" or "in the name of the Father, Son, and Holy Spirit"?

It became clear to me that she'd been made to believe that maybe her baptism "didn't count" or "didn't work." She was worried that she might not be right with God, or that God would reject her if certain words weren't said *precisely* the right way at her baptism. I felt so bad for the poor woman — I wanted to get that weight off her shoulders and ease her mind, so she would know that she was right with God. During our conversation I expressed to her the same thing that Jesus did to the earnest woman in Luke 7:50: "Your faith has saved you — go in peace."

In Matthew 28:19, just before Jesus went back to heaven, He told the apostles to make disciples and baptize them "in the name of the Father and of the Son and of the Holy Spirit." But later, in the Book of the Acts of the Apostles, Peter told a large group of people to repent, and be baptized "in the name of Jesus Christ" (Acts 2:38). Then, in Acts 10:48 (KJV), Peter baptized Cornelius and his family "in the name of the Lord" (Greek: *Kurios*). And we read that some in Samaria and Ephesus were baptized "in the name of the Lord Jesus" (Acts 8:16).

There are Christians who teach that if you're baptized in the name of the Father, Son, and Holy Spirit, then you're not saved; that you can only be saved if you're baptized in Jesus' name. And there are other Christians who say that if you're baptized in Jesus' name, then you're not saved; that you can only be saved if you're baptized in the name of the Father, Son and Holy Spirit. I deliberately wrote it all out like that to give you an idea of how tiring these people are.

What is God's name?

In Exodus 3:13-14, Moses asked God, "What is Your name?"
God replied "My name is *YHVH*" (there are no vowels in Hebrew).
In Psalm 68:4, that name of God is shortened to *Yah* (in English,
with vowels).

In Hebrew the name Jesus is *Yahshua*

Jesus' name, *Yahshua*, has two parts: *Yah*, God's name in Psalm 68:4,
and *shua*, which means savior. Jesus is God our Savior. In Isaiah 9:6,
Jesus is called the Everlasting Father. When you have Jesus, you have
the Father. When you have the Father, you have Jesus. And when
you have the Holy Spirit, you have the Father and Jesus (John 14:23).

 So when Jesus said in Matthew 28:19 to baptize in the
name of the Father and of the Son and of the Holy Spirit,
you could say that *"Jesus" is the name of the Father, and
of the Son, and of the Holy Spirit*. Whether you baptize
"in the name of the Father, Son, and Holy Spirit" or
"in Jesus' name," you're saying the same thing.

What must a person do to be saved?

The answer is — believe in the Lord Jesus Christ. When Jesus said
to baptize them in the name of the Father and the Son and the
Holy Spirit, did He add — *or else they won't be saved*? No, He didn't.
Did He say you must say *these* words, or *any* words while you're
baptizing someone? No, He didn't. Was Jesus saying you must say
these exact words, precisely, with no mistakes, no omissions, or
the baptism won't work? No, He didn't.

So should you be baptized in Jesus' name or in the name of the Father, Son, and Holy Spirit?

It doesn't matter. If you get baptized in the name of the Father, Son
and Holy Spirit, then you're baptized into the name of the Father,
Son, and Holy Spirit. And if you're baptized in Jesus' name you're
baptized into the Father, Son, and Holy Spirit. Why? Because
Colossians 2:9 tells us that everything there is to God is in Jesus.
Jesus is the fullness of God. So when you have Jesus, you have the
Father, the Son, and the Holy Spirit.

Baptism isn't a magic trick

There's no magical incantation that makes it work. The person being baptized needs to understand what the gospel is, who Jesus is, and what baptism represents. They need to be someone who has acknowledged their sinfulness and turned to Jesus to be saved. Those are the words that need to be spoken *before* a person is baptized.

That's what Philip did when he baptized the Ethiopian

Philip made sure the Ethiopian believed in Jesus as his Lord and Savior. But we read of no words, no formula spoken by Philip as he baptized the Ethiopian (Acts 8:35-38).

Which church should I join?

People who took my Quiz were always asking me, "Which church are you with?" And I'd say "I'm not with a church. I do this on my own." It made me realize how grateful I am that I didn't smother my critical thinking and creativity by handing over the reins of my Christian walk to the pastor of a church.

In John 9:1-41, Jesus gave sight to a man who'd been blind from birth. The leaders of that man's church were so angry with jealousy, they told the man he couldn't belong to their church anymore. After the man got kicked out of his church, Jesus came and talked to him. Now what do you think Jesus said to the man? Maybe Jesus told him, "You'd better go back and apologize, and beg them to let you into their church again, because the Bible clearly teaches you must become a member of a local church." No, Jesus didn't say that. Instead, Jesus asked him, "Do you believe in the Son of God?" The man said, "Lord, I believe." Then the man worshipped Jesus. And in doing so, he joined the church (John 9:36-38).

If Jesus didn't tell him the Bible clearly teaches you must become a member of a local church, then why do I keep hearing pastors say that during their sermons? They also mention their PhD in Theology, and tell their listeners they must put themselves under the authority of the elders of their church. There are young, immature seekers who go to those churches with a sincere desire to obey God. They hear that and think, *Yes, I want to obey God so I will join this church and put myself under their authority.* But those babes in Christ aren't mature enough to make that decision. They lack knowledge and discernment. So what that pastor is doing to them is spiritual child abuse. By blindly following his instructions, many become victims of false teachers. A PhD doesn't guarantee that a pastor is called or qualified. A self-educated person might have more understanding of the Bible in their little finger than a PhD has in their whole body (2 Corinthians 11:20).

What is the church?

In Matthew 16:18, Jesus said, "On this rock I will build My church" (Jesus is that Rock). And throughout the New Testament the church is mentioned dozens of times. The Greek word which is translated "church" is *ecclesia*. The word is made up of two parts: *ek*, which means "out from," and *kaleo*, which means "to call." The church, then, is the called-out ones. It is those who have been called out of this world by God to become part of His church. It is all those, all over the world, who belong to Christ. The church is the body of Christ, with Christ as its head in heaven (Ephesians 2:19-22).

The *ecclesia* isn't a local church, and it doesn't need a building. The word has nothing to do with the buildings we know as churches. After Jesus went back to heaven, the apostles didn't build church buildings. Churches as we know them came about after the apostles had all died. Being assembled in a church building is not what makes an *ecclesia*. The *ecclesia* is the Christian people, together in spirit, whether together physically or scattered.

But doesn't Hebrews 13:17 say we must obey church leaders?

We obey the Word of God — which our spiritual leaders are supposed to be teaching us. We put ourselves under the authority of the Word of God, not the person who's teaching the Word. The sheep belong to Jesus, not to the pastor. Jesus told Peter, "Feed *My* sheep," not *your* sheep (John 21:15-17). A good pastor impresses upon people that their own study of the Bible and their personal walk with Christ is most important. When a man does indeed teach the pure Word of God, we should show him respect and help him to keep teaching. But that doesn't mean we wait for him to tell us what to do. A Christian must never let a man replace the leading of the Holy Spirit in their life (Ephesians 4:11-16; 1 Thessalonians 5:12-13; Hebrews 13:7; 1 Peter 2:25; 5:1-4).

Which church should you join?
There's only one church — made up of all those who have the Holy Spirit of God, wherever they may be.

Should Christians worship with people of other religions?

I met beautiful people from various religions in Harvard Square. One of them, a Muslim, told me I was the nicest Christian he'd ever talked to. In the Bible, Jesus tells Christians to love our neighbor with the same love that we feel for ourselves. Jesus meant every neighbor, whether Christian or not.
(Luke 10:25-37; see Leviticus 19:18)

Christians must never take part in a worship service with people of other religions

Isn't that a violation of the command of Jesus to love our neighbor? No. Let me explain. Concerning our salvation, the Bible says:

> There is not another person in the whole world other than Jesus that we must go to for salvation, because there is no salvation in anyone other than Jesus.   - Acts 4:12

And who is Jesus Christ?

- Jesus is Emmanuel, which means "God with us" (Matthew 1:23; see Isaiah 7:14)
- Jesus is the Mighty God, the Everlasting Father (Isaiah 9:6)
- Jesus is God our Savior (Titus 2:13)
- Jesus is the Son of the living God (Matthew 16:16; see Luke 1:30-32)
- Jesus is the Christ, the Messiah, the Anointed One (Luke 4:18)
- Jesus was the sacrifice for sin (1 Peter 1:18-19)
- Jesus rose from the dead (Matthew 28:6)

The divinity, crucifixion, and resurrection of the Lord Jesus Christ are NOT NEGOTIABLE

We were all doomed. But now we have the hope of salvation because God Himself came to earth to be born as a man. He is called Jesus, which means "God, our Savior." He lived a sinless life, died on a cross, rose from death three days later, and went back to heaven. Jesus went to the cross for us because He loves us. Anyone who wants to be saved by Jesus can be, by believing in Him. And whoever believes can be sure that they are saved and will live with Jesus in heaven forever (Romans 10:9; 1 Corinthians 15:1-4; 1 John 4:8; 5:11-13).

Other religions believe in a different Jesus

Other religions say that Jesus was just a man, that He is not God. They say God doesn't have a Son, that Jesus was not crucified, or that He was not raised from the dead. They don't believe that Jesus paid the penalty for sin. They don't believe a person can be saved by believing in Jesus.

I will be faithful to God, my Savior

I want to obey my Lord and Savior Jesus Christ, and love all my neighbors like I love myself. But I can't worship with people of other religions. It's a matter of loyalty to my God. I see it like this: I have my wife. I'm not going to go into the bedroom of my neighbor's wife. I have my God. And I'm not going to go into my neighbor's place of worship (Exodus 23:13; 34:14).

Jesus said:

> *"I am the way, the truth, and the life. No one can get to the Father in any way other than through Me."*
>
> - John 14:6

 If Christians worship with people of other religions, it's like saying those religions are just as good as Christianity. By doing that, Christians are stealing salvation from people of other religions, because they are withholding from them the knowledge that Jesus Christ is the only Savior.

Does a Christian wife have to obey her husband?

Yes, a Christian wife has to obey her husband
Can I prove that? Yes, I can. Ephesians 5:24 says wives must "submit to their husbands in everything." "Submit to" means to obey. First Peter 3:1-6 says a Christian wife should follow the example of Sarah, who "obeyed her husband Abraham and called him lord." Calling a person lord was a way of showing respect (Genesis 18:12).

What does it mean that a wife has to obey her husband?
As with anything in the Bible, this must be interpreted with wisdom which comes from study and prayer. The words "submit to" in Ephesians 5:24 were translated into English from one Greek word: *hupotasso*. It's made up of two parts: *hupo*, which means "under," and *tasso*, which means "to place" (it's like the word *hypodermic*, which is used to describe a needle that's placed under the skin). It means the wife places herself under her husband.

The word *hupotasso* was a military term. In order for the military to do its job there must be those who lead and those who submit to the leaders. *There can't be any infighting.* God is using the example of a military force to teach us how He wants Christians to behave, not just in marriage but in everything. Submission is a Christian virtue. God wants everything done in an orderly fashion.
(Romans 13:1-7; 1 Corinthians 14:33; 15:28; 1 Peter 2:13-18)

Why does the wife have to be the one who submits?
First Corinthians 11:7-9 says:

> The man (husband) is the image and glory of God;
> but the woman (wife) is the glory of man.
> The man didn't come from the woman,
> but the woman came from the man (Genesis 2:7, 21-23);
> and the man wasn't created for the woman,
> but the woman was created for the man (Genesis 2:18).

The roles God gave to husbands and wives are only for this earthly, flesh life. They will disappear in the eternity. Spiritually, we are all the same in God's eyes (Galatians 3:28).

Should a wife ever disobey her husband?
Yes, sometimes a wife *must* disobey her husband. When Ephesians 5:24 says the wife must submit to the husband "in everything" it does not mean in *every* thing. A husband is not to make his wife disobey God's commandments.

First Corinthians 11:3 says that in a Christian marriage the chain of command goes like this: God is the Captain over Christ; Christ is the Captain over the husband; and the husband is the captain over the wife. There could be times when the husband gives an order that goes against the chain of command in such a way that a wife will be found guilty by God if she obeys her husband.

Biblical examples
In Acts 5:1-11, we read about a husband and wife named Ananias and Sapphira who were among the first Christians. The two of them agreed to lie to the apostles about a financial transaction they'd made. The apostle Peter told them they were lying to God's Holy Spirit. As Peter spoke those words to each of them, they dropped dead. Sapphira was just as guilty as Ananias. But what if her heart was different? She could have disobeyed her husband and tried to stop him. Or she could have answered Peter truthfully.

In 1 Samuel 25:1-42, you can read about Abigail, a good woman married to a fool named Nabal. When Nabal acted cruelly to David, God's anointed, Abigail went behind Nabal's back and blessed David and his men. Then God struck Nabal dead and Abigail became David's wife. This tells me that Abigail acted wisely, righteously.

Am I saying wives should disobey their husbands?
I'm saying a Christian wife has God's Holy Spirit, and if the Spirit and the Word of God tell her she must disobey her husband, then she must make a decision.

Why don't wives want to obey their husbands?
Because of the sinful state of our hearts — both men and women. When Adam and Eve disobeyed God they opened the door to death and all kinds of evils. We're just as guilty as they were because we sin too, and we suffer the same consequences they did.

God told Eve that her desire will be to her husband, and her husband will rule over her (Genesis 3:16). The word "desire" is the same word used in Genesis 4:7 when God told Cain that sin's "desire" will be to him, but he must rule over it. It means that in her fallen, sinful state, the wife wants to control her husband. The husband wants to control the wife, but in his fallen, sinful state, he wants to control her in selfish ways. That's where we get the battle of the sexes, and why there's so much divorce.

What does God want the husband to do?
God tells Christian husbands:

> Love your wives even as Christ also loved the church,
> and gave Himself for the church.   - Ephesians 5:25

How did Christ give Himself for the church? He died for her, painfully. God's making a point here — love your wife that much. God said it's the husband's duty, the debt he owes. A husband needs to love his wife — whether he feels like it or not, on good days and bad, whether he think she deserves it or not. Really?

Yes. First John 4:19 says the church loves Christ because Christ loved us first. And if the husband is to obey God and love his wife like Christ loved the church, then he must love his wife first, no matter what. Colossians 3:19 says husbands are not to subject their wives to bitterness or resentment. In Ephesians 5:28-29 and 33, God told husbands they are to love their wives like they love their own body (Matthew 19:3-6). God said no one hates their own body. We love our bodies by giving them good nourishing food, warmth and care. God said a husband must let his wife know he appreciates her. He is to treasure her, take pleasure in her, let her know how valuable she is, uplift her, and cherish her (Proverbs 5:18-19; Song of Solomon 2:3-6; 5:16).

How can a Christian husband and wife make it work?
Look at what God has told the husband to do. Who has the greater responsibility? Who gives themselves the most? It's the husband.

Ephesians 5:23 says the husband is the captain of the wife as Christ is the Captain of the church. The church submits to and obeys Christ, but what did Christ do? He humbled Himself to wash the feet of the apostles who represented the church. Jesus did it to teach us that He is the only one who can wash us of our sins, and to teach Christians how we are to relate to one another (John 13:4-5; Ephesians 5:1-2).

 Should a husband be that humble toward his wife?
Yes. Then it will be easy for a wife to submit. It will be a joy.

She doesn't submit by force, but in response to her husband's love and out of a duty to God. When the husband shows love to his wife, he gives her the ability to obey God by submitting to her husband. That will be a great blessing to both of them. The love between a Christian husband and wife is based on mutual respect. God didn't make the husband captain over his wife so he could have a maid or a sex slave.

What is God's ultimate purpose in this?
God commands it because it's what's best for His plan of salvation. Even Jesus, who is God Himself, submitted to the will of the Father so that the plan of salvation could be carried out (Philippians 2:5-8).

God hasn't left us on our own; He is with the Christian husband and wife. God tells us in Ephesians 5:18-19 to walk in the Spirit, His Holy Spirit. And we do that by staying in His Word, studying the Bible. A Christian husband and wife talk about what they've learned from the Bible as they walk down the street and at dinnertime. That's their part, what they do. And in return, God will give them the strength, the ability, faith, and love, to serve Him in their proper roles. Then they can do their work of sharing the gospel. Jesus put aside His glory to do God's will, and both the husband and the wife put aside their own selfish desires in order to obey God and do His will.

Is a divorced Christian free to remarry?

A young woman with a small child came up to me at the Quiz and said she was divorced. She wept as she told me how lonely she was, and how hard it was being a single mother. I asked her if she'd considered trying marriage again, and she said, "No, the Bible doesn't permit divorced Christians to get married again." I tried to convince her that she was mistaken but I couldn't, and the poor woman went away sad. If the Bible *does* permit this woman to remarry, shouldn't she be told, so she can find a companion, a father for her child, and happiness instead of sadness?

In Deuteronomy 24:1, God said that if a husband finds *some uncleanness* in his wife he may give her a bill of divorcement. The expression "some uncleanness" means obscene nakedness. It means the wife was unfaithful to her husband by committing a sin of a sexual nature.

The Pharisees were religious leaders, as well as hypocrites, serial sinners, unrepentant, hardhearted, unloving, selfish, and cruel. They misused Scripture, and added their own rules alongside God's laws. In Matthew 19:3, when the Pharisees questioned Jesus, they claimed that Deuteronomy 24:1 gave permission for a man to divorce his wife for *any reason.* They were using that perversion of Scripture as an excuse to get rid of a wife they were tired of, and marry a woman they lusted after. They used Deuteronomy 24:1 for sinful purposes.

The Pharisees went against the intent of that verse. We always have to look at the intent of a passage of Scripture. What Jesus said in Matthew 5:31-32, 19:3-9, and Luke 16:18, was directed at the Pharisees. Jesus made His point by saying that if a man divorces his wife *not* because of "some uncleanness" but for "any reason," then the divorce isn't valid and they are still married. So if the woman remarried, then the man who married her was committing adultery.

But Jesus did not say those things to sentence divorced women to a life of loneliness. Jesus is the great defender of women.

God didn't divorce His wife just for *any reason,* and neither should a man (Jeremiah 3:8). Marriage is meant to be for life. But what if divorce happens?

Free to remarry

Which brings us back to the young woman who came to me at the Quiz. What if her divorce was all her fault; what if she divorced because of her own sinfulness? Remember Deuteronomy 24:1? It says the husband can divorce the wife if he finds some uncleanness in her. Well, the very next verse says that the wife who is given the bill of divorcement and sent away, is then free to remarry.

First Corinthians 6:16 says that if a man sins by lying down with a prostitute, then he and that prostitute become one flesh. That's the same expression Jesus used when He said that in marriage a man and woman become one flesh. It's as though the prostitute is marrying every man she sleeps with. But what if she repents of her prostitution and turns to Jesus? The Bible says that those who turn to Jesus will be completely forgiven for *all* their sins (Mark 3:28; Titus 2:13-14; 1 John 1:9).

 That young divorced woman is a Christian.
When she repents of any sin she may have committed in getting divorced, then it's like it never happened. *She is washed clean, she gets a new start. She is free to remarry* (Psalm 51:7; 103:12; Isaiah 1:18; 38:17; 43:25; Hebrews 8:12).

Are Christians hypocrites?

Skeptics think Christians are hypocrites, and that vexes the skeptic's sense of morality. But from God's point of view, it's the skeptic who's the hypocrite.

> A young man came up to the Quiz, looked at my pamphlets, and told me, "Jesus said 'Don't judge.'"
> I replied, "Yes, Jesus did say 'Don't judge,' but He was telling *hypocrites* not to judge."
> The young man said, "We're all hypocrites."
> And I replied, "No, if we were *all* hypocrites then Jesus would have said, 'Don't judge,' and stopped there."

But Jesus didn't stop there. He went on to give a vivid illustration using a splinter and a log to show how a hypocrite thinks. Jesus said the hypocrite always wants to judge and fix someone else's small sin [splinter] while ignoring their own large sin [log] (Matthew 7:1-5).

Jesus said the hypocrite needs to fix their log before they can judge and fix someone's splinter. How do you fix the log? Acknowledge that the log exists and turn to Jesus Christ so He can forgive you and cleanse you (1 John 1:9).

Right after Jesus told hypocrites they must never judge, He told Christians that we *must* judge (Matthew 7:6). Jesus said Christians are never to give His valuable teachings to dogs and pigs.

Yes, Jesus compared certain people to dogs and pigs. If you give a valuable object to a dog or a pig, will they recognize it as valuable? No, they will tear it to pieces and stomp on it. Jesus doesn't want His truths or His messengers torn to pieces and stomped on. Now tell me, please, how in the world are you going to know who's a dog or a pig without judging? Do you see what Jesus cleverly did there?

He gave *context* to His teachings about "not judging" (Matthew 7:15-20; Revelation 2:2,6)

What about the skeptic's argument that Christians are hypocrites because we teach morality and yet we still sin? Yes, Christians sin, but that doesn't mean we're hypocrites. If you want to know what a hypocrite is, then look at the religious leaders called Pharisees.

The Pharisees were doing that splinter and log thing. They made up endless rules and forced the people to obey them. But the Pharisees ignored their own cruelty and hatred of others. The Pharisees were into external shows of religious performance: *Look at me, I'm praying, I'm fasting, I'm so holy.* Jesus said they were like tombs that appear beautiful on the outside but on the inside are full of dead people's bones and filth (Matthew 6:1-5; 16-18; 23:1-36; Mark 7:6-9).

Hypocrites are not made in a day
The Pharisees were career hypocrites. They rejected Christ.
They preferred their own so-called righteousness.
Christians don't pretend to be righteous.
We cling to God's morality; we cling to our Bibles
(Luke 16:15; Philippians 3:9).

 A Christian has something the skeptic doesn't have. Christians have the righteousness of Christ because we believe in Jesus, confess our sins, and ask God to forgive us. Then we're 100% righteous, and that's something no skeptic can ever be (Luke 18:9-14; 1 John 1:7; Revelation 1:5).

Like the Pharisees, the skeptic has rejected the righteousness of Christ. The skeptic is only pretending to be righteous, because without Jesus you don't have righteousness. That's why God sees the skeptic as the hypocrite, not the Christian.

Can a Christian lose their salvation?

No, a Christian cannot lose their salvation, never ever. But what about people who are Christians and quit, become atheists, and even attack the faith? The apostle John addressed that in 1 John 2:19. There are people who appear to be Christians, externally. They go through the motions and say the right things, but then they leave and that's it. They abandon the faith, they move on, and then we can see who they really were on the inside. John said those who do that were never Christians to begin with. If they *were* Christians, they would have continued on. They're referred to in John 15:1-6; Hebrews 6:4-6 and 10:29; 2 Peter 2:1-3 and 20-22; and Jude 1:3-4.

But if you sincerely believe in, love, and follow the Lord Jesus Christ, then you can rest assured, your soul is kept safe in His hands.

> "Everyone that the Father gives Me will come to Me. *And I will never throw them out.* Because the desire of the One who sent Me is that I won't lose any of the ones He has given Me; but I will raise them up on the last day. This is indeed My Father's desire. Whoever looks to the Son and believes in Him will have eternal life, and I will raise them up on the last day."
>
> - Jesus, John 6:37, 39-40

 > "My sheep hear My voice, and I know them, and they follow Me. I give them eternal life and they will never perish. *And no one will ever take them from My hand.* My Father who gave them to Me is greater than everyone, and no one can take them from my Father's hand. I and My Father are one."
>
> - Jesus, John 10:27-30

Romans 8:9 says that if you have the Holy Spirit, you belong to Christ. And in John 14:16, Jesus says that when He and the Father come to live in your heart, they will stay with you forever (Philippians 1:6; 1 Peter 1:3-5)

Chapter Eight

What did Jesus mean?

Be a person who's always thinking, When can I run back to my Bible so I can dig into God's truths again?

Then, because of your hard work, you'll learn how to put each truth from the Bible in its proper place. You won't put things where they don't belong.

And when you present yourself to God for inspection you won't feel ashamed, you'll be confident, knowing that God will say to you,"Well done, My good and faithful servant."

- 2 Timothy 2:15; Matthew 25:21a

"It's easier for a camel to go through the eye of a needle than for a rich man to get into the kingdom of God"

 Jesus meant that when the things money can buy are *most* important to a person, they will find it very difficult to get into heaven.

Jesus had just finished talking to a man who chose his money instead of following Jesus (Matthew 19:22). After the man walked away, Jesus turned to His disciples and told them that people who *trust in their money* find the obedience required to enter the kingdom of heaven to be distasteful (Mark 10:24, KJV). It was then that Jesus said, "It's easier for a camel to go through the eye of a needle than for a rich man to enter the kingdom of God." Jesus was talking about people like that rich man whose heart was set on the things of this world. It's no sin to be rich as long as our heart is in heaven, and we follow it there (Proverbs 11:28; Matthew 6:21; Luke 12:13-21).

Didn't Jesus say "Woe unto you that are rich"?

Yes, Jesus said, "Woe unto you that are rich,"and in the very next verse He said, "Woe unto you that laugh now" (Luke 6:24-25). "Woe" is like saying, "You're doomed, you poor fools." Is it a sin to laugh? Of course not. Just like it's not a sin to be rich. We have to look at the context. Just before Jesus said those words, He told His disciples to be very happy because they'd chosen Jesus instead of the fleeting pleasures of this world. They hungered for what is right and cried tears of sorrow because of the evil things being done in the world. They were hated because they did the work of a disciple of Jesus. And Jesus told them to jump for joy because of what awaited them in heaven (Luke 6:20-23).

So Jesus said woe to those who want to be rich and laugh, while having nothing to do with Jesus. They ignore the things of heaven and just enjoy the pleasures of this world.

"You must hate your father and mother"

A man came up to me in Harvard Square and said, "I'm Hindu. I want you to know I respect Jesus." I said, "Thank you," and we shook hands. And then he said, "But I have a question. Why did Jesus say you must hate your mother and father?"

In Luke 14:25-26, when a multitude of people gathered around Jesus to hear from Him, He said, "If you don't hate your father and mother, then you can't follow Me." But in Matthew 15:4, Jesus quoted the fifth commandment which says to honor your parents or suffer severe consequences (Exodus 20:12). Did Jesus contradict Himself? No, because when Jesus said you must hate your father and mother, He didn't mean you must hate your father and mother. So, then He must have changed the definition of the word "hate," right? No, He meant hate in it's usual meaning, hate in the strongest possible sense.

So, what did Jesus mean? In Matthew 10:34-37, Jesus said He came not to bring peace on earth, but war:

> "And a person's enemies will be the members of his own
> family. Whoever loves their father or mother more than
> they love Me is not worthy to follow Me."   - Matthew 10:37

Jesus said you must hate your father and mother as a way to warn you that when you become a Christian you could be pressured by family members to quit. Jesus wants you to love your parents but give all your heart to Him.

 He meant don't let them pull you away, stay loyal to Him.

It's like if someone is very hungry. They could say, "I'm hungry," or "I'm really hungry." But you'd really get it if they said, "I'm so hungry I could eat a horse."

"Believers will pick up deadly snakes and drink poison"

In Mark 16:18, Jesus said that those who believe in Him will take up serpents (snakes) with their hands, and if they drink poison it won't hurt them. There are people who think Jesus wants them to pick up rattlesnakes and drink poison. If they do that, they could be guilty of murdering themselves and anyone else who follows them.

Jesus said we must never test God by doing foolish things. And God said, "Do not commit murder." Jesus would never tell us to do something that would cause us to disobey God. So Jesus could not possibly have been telling us to *literally*, actually, pick up rattlesnakes or drink poison (Exodus 20:13; Matthew 4:7).

If Jesus *was* giving an order, telling His followers who walked with Him to pick up snakes and drink poison, then every one of His followers disobeyed that order. There is not one who drank poison on purpose or even accidentally. None of the disciples of Jesus ever deliberately picked up a snake. The apostle Paul was bitten by a poisonous snake, but it was an accident. Paul didn't even see the snake until its fangs were fastened onto his hand. And Paul wasn't hurt by the snake's poisonous venom. He shook the snake off his hand and went on (Acts 28:1-6).

There's no way anyone can make a case based on *one incident* that Jesus had been talking about literal snakes or literal poison. And you can't make a case that Christians should be literally picking up snakes because Paul survived being bitten by a poisonous snake. That was Paul. Paul was special, he was an apostle. Sick people were healed when they came into contact with napkins that touched Paul's skin. Think about *that* before you try picking up a poisonous snake. We're not Paul, we're not apostles (Acts 19:11-12; 20:9-12; 28:8-9).

So if Jesus didn't mean it literally, then He meant it *figuratively*
Can we find evidence in the Bible to show that snakes and poison could be used figuratively? Yes, we can. In Luke 10:17-19, the disciples told Jesus that when they acted under His power and authority, evil spirits were stripped of their power. Jesus told them He had given them power to stomp on serpents and scorpions, and over all the power of the enemy. The Enemy is the devil. And the "serpents" and "scorpions" that Jesus referred to are evil spirits that are under the power of the devil and do his evil deeds. Those are the figurative poisonous snakes that Jesus was referring to. But how do we pick them up with our hands? (Matthew 13:39; Revelation 20:2).

When Jesus said in Mark 16:18 that those who believe in Him will "take up" serpents with their hands, it means to lift up and remove them. It's what the disciples did in Luke 10:17-19 (above). By the authority of Jesus Christ, they removed the evil spirits by stripping them of their power. And the hand is used figuratively in the Bible to refer to a person's ability and actions (1 Chronicles 29:12; Psalm 31:15; 118:15-17).

  When the disciples "took up serpents with their hands"
they removed the evil spirits' power with the power of Jesus.

When Jesus said that if His followers drink anything poisonous they won't be hurt by it, He didn't mean a poisonous liquid — He was speaking *figuratively*. Romans 3:13 says that the enemies of Christians speak fraudulent words, and the poison of venomous snakes is under their lips. Here, "poison" is used to show how evil their intentions are.

  The poison under their lips is the cursing, lies, slander,
and insults they hurl at Christians. But Jesus said their
venom won't hurt us. We have Jesus, so we have the
ultimate victory over the devil and his evil workers
(Deuteronomy 20:4; Psalm 140:1-7; Revelation 19:20).

"He that is without sin, cast the first stone"

This saying has been used to make people think that calling something sinful is a worse sin than the sin itself.

I have two questions for you.
First question: Have you ever done anything wrong?
Is your answer... "Yes"?
Second question: Is it wrong for a man to rape a woman?
I'll assume your answer is again, "Yes."

So tell me, where do you get the nerve to say it's wrong for a man to rape a woman, when *you've* done wrong? [An absurd question, because rape is wrong — period.] But that's how people use the words of Jesus, "He that is without sin, cast the first stone" (John 8:7).

Was Jesus saying you can't judge something to be wrong unless you're sinless? That's impossible. Why? Because if that's what Jesus was saying, then He would be contradicting the Bible, contradicting Himself, and Jesus doesn't do that. There is not one believer who is without sin, but Jesus *praised* believers who examined Bible teachers to find out which ones are liars. The Bible *commands* believers to be witnesses in a court of law; to mark and avoid those who harm the flock; and to judge, hate, and expose the work of false teachers.
(Numbers 35:30; Romans 16:17; 1 Corinthians 5:11; Revelation 2:2,6)

To find out what Jesus *did* mean, let's look closely at the incident in John 8:1-11 which caused Jesus to utter that saying. One morning while Jesus was teaching the people, He was interrupted by some Pharisees, religious authorities. They'd brought a woman with them. They said to Jesus:

> "Teacher, this woman was caught committing adultery, in the
> very act. The law of Moses commands us that such should be
> stoned to death. What do *You* say?"   - John 8:4-5

It was a set-up:

1) John 8:6 tells us the Pharisees were only doing this to try and trap Jesus. As a teacher of Israel, if Jesus said, "Don't stone her," He could be accused of disobeying the law of Moses and be killed like Stephen was. And if Jesus said, "Stone her," then He could be killed by the Roman government for rebellion, because only they had the authority to execute people (John 18:31; Acts 6:11).

2) The law of Moses commanded that both the man and the woman were to be stoned for adultery. The Pharisees only brought the woman (Deuteronomy 22:22).

The law of Moses said that in a case which called for the death penalty, there must be two people who could testify that they witnessed the crime, and these two witnesses must cast the first stone at the guilty person (Deuteronomy 17:6-7).

Jesus brilliantly escaped their trap and turned it on them, by also citing the law of Moses which said that as the woman's accusers, *they* would have to cast the first stone to kill her. Jesus used the saying "He that is without sin, cast the first stone" to cut to their hearts, and make them face the sinfulness of what they were doing with this set-up.

Jesus knew they never intended to stone the woman. *He called their bluff* to force the situation to a conclusion. And it worked, because they just scurried off.

So that saying of Jesus is only for cases like this one — fraudulent cases. *Jesus was not saying that only sinless people can judge something to be wrong.* Jesus loves true judgment and justice, but He hates hypocrisy (Matthew 23:13-29).

"Turn the other cheek"

I know a young woman who has just gotten interested in the Bible for the first time, so she knows next to nothing about the Christian faith. A Christian man told her Jesus said that if somebody slaps her on her cheek, she should let them slap her other cheek too. He made it sound as though Jesus wants Christians to just let someone beat them to death.

If somebody physically attacks you — or others — Jesus does NOT want you to turn your other cheek to them. Self-defense is a God-given duty, and shirking it is a sin (Proverbs 24:11-12).

"Whosoever shall rape thy wife, give to him thy daughter also" … (!)

— that's what some people think Jesus meant when He said:
"Whosoever shall smite thee on thy right cheek, turn to him the other also."
- Matthew 5:39 (KJV)

So what *did* Jesus mean?

 You've heard people say, "Wow, that was a real slap in the face." It's an expression. It means someone insulted you and it hurts like a slap in the face. It stings, and your initial reaction is to insult them back, but Jesus says, *don't do it, let the insult pass.* That's what Jesus meant by "turn the other cheek." He was just talking about insults, not about physical assaults.

But didn't Jesus rebuke Peter, telling him that "those who live by the sword shall perish by the sword"? NO. Let's look at what really happened. I want you to know the truth, because it literally is a matter of life and death.

Peter drew a sword and struck a man named Malchus.
Then Jesus said to Peter:

> "You've done enough, put your sword back in its holster.
> I accept the fate My Father has given Me. If I asked, He
> would instantly give Me more than 70,000 angels to protect
> me. But then how would the Scriptures be fulfilled? All those
> who have taken the sword shall perish by the sword."
> - Matthew 26:52-54; Luke 22:51; John 18:11

1) **Notice, Jesus didn't say, "Peter! Get rid of that detestable
    weapon!"** Do you know why? It's because Jesus was the one
    who told Peter to buy that sword. In fact, having a sword was
    so important that Jesus told Peter if he didn't have the money to
    buy a sword, he should sell his coat to get one. Jesus didn't tell
    Peter to go bury the sword somewhere. He told Peter to put it
    back in its holster. He let Peter keep the sword (Luke 22:36).

2) **Why did Peter draw the sword and strike Malchus?** Because
    Peter wanted to protect Jesus. We are told in Matthew 26:50
    that men came to take Jesus away, and that they "laid hands
    on Jesus." If Jesus *hadn't* stopped Peter from doing more,
    then Peter would have ended up dead too. Jesus even healed
    Malchus of the wound Peter had given him, to make sure that
    Peter wouldn't be killed. Jesus still had work for Peter to do.
    It wasn't Peter's time to die (John 21:18-19; 2 Peter 1:13-15).

3) **When Jesus told Peter "those who take the sword will
    perish by the sword," Jesus wasn't talking about Peter.** What
    did Jesus call the men who laid hands on Him? He said, "The
    Son of Man is betrayed into the hands of sinners." And what
    were those sinners carrying when they came for Jesus? Swords!
    They were the ones taking the sword, *they* were the ones who
    would perish by the sword — because they wanted to murder
    Jesus. Peter wasn't going to perish — Peter loved Jesus.
    (Matthew 26:45,47,55; John 21:15-17)

Jesus does not forbid self-defense

"I was hungry and you fed me"

Some Christians create a false gospel out of their shallow interpretation of this saying.

If, as a result of reading these words of Jesus, you decide to devote yourself to working at the local soup kitchen, then you need to dig deeper into your Bible.

It doesn't help that non-Christian skeptics are always accusing Christians by saying we aren't following Jesus because we're hung up on "issues" when we should be out helping the poor. Then there's the bad pastors who tell eager, compassionate Christians that Jesus wants then to work in soup kitchens in order to save their souls. And there's the socialists in Christian clothing.

Here's what Jesus said:

> "I was hungry and you gave Me something to eat;
> I was thirsty and you gave Me drink;
> I was a stranger, and you took Me in;
> naked, and you covered Me;
> I was without strength and you nursed Me back to health;
> I was in prison and you visited Me."
>
> - Matthew 25:35-36

In Matthew 25:40, Jesus explained that you did those things to Him when you did them to even the most humble one of His brethren.

Here the word "brethren" means both brother and sisters, and Romans 8:29 says that Jesus is the firstborn among many brethren. In an Israelite family, the firstborn male was highest in rank among his brethren, so Jesus is highest in rank among His brothers and sisters, which include all Christians.

So what *does* Jesus want you to do to Christians, His brethren?
Look at two other things Jesus said:

In Matthew 5:6, Jesus talked about a person who hungers and thirsts, but not for food and drink. This person hungers and thirsts for God's righteousness. Jesus said this person is supremely happy and fortunate because they shall be satisfied.

In John 4:14, Jesus said if a person drinks from the water that He will give them, they will never thirst because the water that He gives is a fountain of water bubbling up into eternal life.

 How do we give *that* food and drink to the Christian brethren? By sharing the Bible, teaching the word of God. You can give someone a sandwich but tomorrow they'll be hungry again. Or you can give them the Word of God which is the Bread of Life, the Living Water that leads to eternal life and gives them God's Holy Spirit.

Jesus has many brethren out there who are like lost sheep
They haven't come home to Him yet. We don't rescue them by working in soup kitchens but by obeying Jesus and teaching the Bible, and doing what Jesus said to do in Matthew 25:35-36:

- Taking into Christian fellowship those who are strangers to God's promises (Ephesians 2:12).

- Covering their sins with the sacrifice of Jesus on the cross (Romans 4:7).

- Nursing those who are without strength because of sin (Romans 5:6; 1 Thessalonians 2:7).

- Visiting those who are being held by the devil in the prison of sin and death, and freeing them (Isaiah 61:1; Hebrews 2:14-15).

"It's not what goes into a person's mouth that defiles them"

When you get to Mark 7:19 in most translations of the Bible, you're told that Jesus made an amazing announcement. Remember back in the Old Testament when God said His people must not eat certain animals and when they do eat them He finds it to be disgusting? Well, guess what, Jesus said, "Never mind." Yes, it seems Jesus suddenly decided it's not disgusting to eat those animals after all. Some Bible versions even tell us that Jesus purified those animals so we could eat them. Most likely, your church also teaches you that Jesus said it's okay now to eat pigs and all the other animals God said not to eat (Leviticus 11:1-47). I'm going to prove to you that those Bible translations and your church are wrong.

Will they blame Jesus for the Tide pod challenge?

If you take the saying of Jesus, "It's not what goes into a person's mouth that defiles them" out of the Bible and separate it from the words Jesus said before and after that saying, then you can claim it means anything you want it to. Why stop at food? Maybe Jesus meant it's okay to put a Tide pod in your mouth. Do you see then how ridiculous and dangerous it is to misuse the words of Jesus? The only way you can learn what Jesus meant is by making the effort to do the hard work of studying not only the passage where Jesus said those words, but by studying the entire Bible with wisdom from God. That saying of Jesus is recorded in Matthew 15:1-20 and Mark 7:1-23.

Who did Jesus say those words to, and why?

Jesus said them to the Pharisees who were the religious leaders of His day. They saw themselves as so holy and everyone else so spiritually dirty, that when they got home after being in public they felt defiled. So the Pharisees made up a handwashing ritual they thought would make them completely holy again. They wouldn't eat until they performed the ritual. When they noticed that the disciples of Jesus didn't do the ritual before they ate, they asked Jesus why.

The difference between Jesus and the Pharisees

Jesus loved the people and the Pharisees didn't. The Pharisees were oppressing the people by making them observe their phony rules like the handwashing ritual. When the Pharisees asked Jesus why His disciples didn't perform the ritual, Jesus used that as an opportunity to rebuke the Pharisees and liberate the people from their tyranny.

 Here's what Jesus meant by the saying:
In Matthew 15:20, Jesus told the people that eating without first doing the handwashing ritual of the Pharisees will NOT cause a person to be spiritually defiled. That, and *only that*, is what Jesus was talking about when He said, "It's not what goes into a person's mouth that defiles them."

Peter understood. The apostle Peter knew Jesus didn't mean it was okay to eat pork. Later on, after Jesus went back to heaven, Peter was presented with a sheet in a vision, on which were animals that God had said not to eat, such as pigs. Peter was told to eat them. But Peter refused to eat them and said he had *never* eaten such things (Acts 10:14). To learn the meaning of the vision, see "What's the cure for racism?" page 191.

Jesus didn't do what He rebuked the Pharisees for doing
Jesus told the Pharisees that by making up their own rules and forcing the people to obey them, they were rejecting the authority of the Bible (Matthew 15:6; Mark 7:13). *Now do you think Jesus Himself would then turn around and reject the authority of the Bible* by telling people they can disregard God's commandment to avoid eating animals such as pigs? No, of course not; Jesus wouldn't do that.

Jesus taught respect for God's law

Jesus had harsh warnings for those who treat God's law as a light thing (Matthew 5:17-20; 7:21-23; Luke 8:21; 11:28):

> *"Anyone who rejects the authority of the least of God's commandments, and teaches people to do the same, shall be called the least in the kingdom of heaven."* - Matthew 5:19

"You are poor but you are rich"

Who did Jesus say was rich, but poor?

Jesus told the Christians of the church in Laodicea He found their indifference so disgusting He would turn His back on them if they didn't repent. Why? Because they said, "I've made myself rich and I'm not lacking anything" (Revelation 3:14-17). But Jesus sarcastically told them:

> "What you fail to understand is that you are beaten-down, desperate, poverty-stricken, blind, and insufficiently dressed. I'm advising you to consider a new plan. I know how fond you are of buying things. So it's time you started 'buying' from Me. I can 'sell' you gold that's been purified by fire that will make you rich. I'll 'sell' you white garments to cover up the disgrace of your nakedness and be sufficiently clothed. And I'll 'sell' you eyewash to rub in your eyes so you'll be able to see."
>
> - Revelation 3:17-18

Do you need money to buy from Jesus?

No. Isaiah 55:1 says, "Everyone listen! I have great news for those of you who thirst. Come to the waters! Those of you who have no money can come and buy, and eat. Come and buy wine with no money and buy milk with no cash."

Who did Jesus say was poor, but rich?

Jesus told the Christians of the church in Smyrna that they were poor — but they were rich. Smyrna is the persecuted church. They're the Christians who boldly proclaim the truths of the Bible. As a result they're so persecuted they have everything taken from them and have to subsist on charity. Jesus told them He was aware of their poverty. But then Jesus said to them, "You are rich." The Christians of Smyrna have the spiritual riches the Laodiceans lack (Revelation 2:8-10).

 Oh, the depth of the riches of the wisdom and knowledge of God!

- Romans 11:33

Chapter Nine

Life
and death

Teach us that life is short,
so we will choose to live wisely.

- Psalm 90:12

What's God got against sex?

How can young people be sexually pure if we take the Bible away from them? That's like asking them to grow tomato plants but telling them they can't have any water.

There's a very important thing I want you to know

You never have to have sex if you don't want to — no matter how much someone pressures you. You are in charge of your body.

Let me tell you about Joseph, one of my favorite people in the Old Testament. Joseph was a beautiful young man with an athletic body. He worked for a man who treated him well, but the man's wife began looking lustfully at Joseph. One day she said to him, "Come and sleep with me."

But Joseph refused. He said, "Your husband trusts me completely; none of his employees has more authority then me. He has held back nothing from me — except you, because you are his wife. How could I do such a wicked thing? It would be a great sin against God."

She kept pressuring Joseph day after day, but he refused to sleep with her, and he kept out of her way as much as possible. One day while Joseph was doing his work and no one was around, she grabbed hold of his shirt and demanded that he go to bed with her. But Joseph tore himself away from her even as she held on to his shirt until the shirt was ripped from his body. Joseph ran off as she held his shirt in her hand (Genesis 39:1-12).

Joseph stayed faithful to God's standards. They never change, as we read in the following New Testament passage:

God didn't give you a physical body so you could use it for unlawful sexual activity. Your body is to be used to do the work God wants you to do ...

And your body is meant to be a place where God dwells.
Run away from unlawful sexual activity!

- 1 Corinthians 6:13-20

Joseph knew right from wrong. As a child of Israel, he would have been taught God's laws. But it's not easy to resist sexual temptation, especially when you're young. Why was Joseph able to resist? Joseph resisted because God was with him (Genesis 39:2,23).

Let me ask you a question:
Do you want to sin sexually in disobedience to God?

If you do, then go home, take your Bible, put it in a drawer and leave it there. My point is, if you want God to be with you like He was with Joseph, you've got to study your Bible. Fill it up with notes, carry it with you wherever you go, think about, talk about, and write about what you learn.

If you do those things, believing in Jesus and following Him, then do you know what you'll be doing? You'll be walking in the Spirit — God's Spirit, the Holy Spirit. And that Spirit is the living water which will give you spiritual nourishment, strength, and life. But without walking in the Spirit you'll be like tomatoes that are dying on the vine because they weren't watered (John 7:37-39; compare Ephesians 5:18-19 with Colossians 3:16).

King David wrote:

> *How can a young person stay pure?*
> *By obeying God's Word. I look for You, Lord:*
> *don't let me wander from Your commandments.*
> *I have hidden Your Word in my heart so that I will*
> *not sin against You.*

- Psalm 119:9-11

God's got nothing against sex. He created it for our enjoyment and so we could produce children. But God wants us to be sexually pure, which means obeying His laws regarding sex. God doesn't permit unmarried men and women to engage in sexual relations. *The only sexual relationship that is blessed by God is between one man and one woman who marry for life.*

Jesus said:

"Don't you know what the Scriptures say? From the beginning God made male and female."
- Matthew 19:4

Then Jesus quoted Genesis 2:24:

"That's why a man leaves his father and mother, and is joined with his wife so that the two of them become one flesh."
- Matthew 19:5

Jesus added:

"No one is allowed to take apart what God has put together."
- Matthew 19:6

God is deadly serious about sex. In Mark 7:21, Jesus said that unlawful sexual activity — called *porneia* in Greek — is an evil that comes from the heart. You can find some of God's definitions of unlawful sexual activities in Exodus 20:14, Leviticus 18:6-17; 20:13-16, and Deuteronomy 22:25-27; 23:18.

If we disobey God's laws and stray from the moral guidelines He's given us in the Bible, we will suffer serious consequences. In Deuteronomy 28:1-68, God explains that blessings come to those who obey His laws but miseries come upon those who disobey them. A great majority of people who are sexually active outside of marriage have sexually transmitted diseases, STDs, which can be incurable, painful, and sometimes fatal. You can get them even if you use protection. You might think you don't care — you just want to enjoy sex. But you'll regret it later if you get sick. And you'll have to face God to be judged (Exodus 15:26; Romans 2:5-6).

In Galatians 6:7-8, God said:

> Don't fool yourself — you can't mock God. You will reap
> what you sow. Those who live only to satisfy their own sinful
> desires will reap decay and death. But those who live to please
> God will reap everlasting life from walking in His Spirit.

If you follow God's way and only have sex in a faithful Christian
marriage, you'll be pleasing to God. You'll have happiness, joy, peace
of mind, and you'll protect your health.
(Proverbs 3:1-2, 7-8; 8:32-35; 1 Peter 2:11; 4:1-7)

First Thessalonians 4:3-4 says God wants us to take control over our
body and run away from any sexual activity that is contrary to His
laws. Two verses later, God said we must never take advantage of
someone. If we engage in unlawful sex, God says we're doing wrong
to the other person, and He holds us accountable for leading them
astray. In fact, we are lying to them because we're withholding the
truth from them that it's unlawful. God says this makes Him angry
and He will bring a severe judgment on us. Even if the other person
is an adult and consenting, they are God's child.
(Romans 1:18; 1 Thessalonians 4:5-6)

 Why a man and a woman?
The reason God is so angry about unlawful sexual
activities and punishes them severely, is because
marriage between one man and one woman symbolizes
the spiritual marriage between Jesus Christ and His Church.
Unlawful sexual relations desecrate that symbolism.

(Matthew 22:1-14; 25:1-13; 2 Corinthians 11:2; Ephesians 5:25,32; Revelation 19:6-9)

God said, "Be holy" and He wouldn't have said it if it was impossible
to be pure. You can live a sexually pure life at any age if you have
God's Holy Spirit. And if you feel tempted to give in, remember what
Jesus went through to pay the penalty for our sins.

When someone tries to pressure you to have sex, set your face like a rock and say, "No! In Jesus' name — go away!" Jesus gave His life to free us from sin, clean us up, and make us His very own people who are eager to do what's right. Let's cling to our Bibles and strive for purity, without which no one will see the Lord (Romans 8:13; 12:1-2; Titus 2:14; Hebrews 12:14; 1 Peter 1:15; 2:11; 4:1-7).

What do I do if I mess up?
You got saved, got baptized, and then what happened? You sinned. Does it mean you're not really saved? No, it means you're human. Don't be shocked. We sin — you're no different. That's why Jesus had to save us. We won't be 100% free of sin until Jesus returns and gives us our eternal spiritual body.

The question is — what are you going to do about it? If you acknowledge your sin, go to God, and ask Him to forgive you in Jesus' name, then He will — and you'll be clean. First John 1:8-10 says that if we claim we don't sin, we're just fooling ourselves and living a lie. But if we tell God that we sinned, He is faithful and good, and He will forgive us and cleanse us.

What if you're a young person who's not married, and you notice that a person of the opposite sex is attractive? That's a blessing from God. It's natural and good. Thank God for that.

What does the Bible say about children in the womb?

God chose a medical doctor named Luke (Colossians 4:14) to record the births of John the Baptist and Jesus. When John was in his mother's womb he was referred to as a baby (Luke 1:44). The word Luke used for "baby" is the Greek word *brephos*. After Jesus was born and was being held by His mother, Luke referred to Jesus as a baby and used the same Greek word, *brephos* (Luke 2:12). John was in his mother's womb and Jesus was a newborn infant, but Luke called both of them *brephos*, meaning baby.

Do children in the womb feel emotions?

A virgin named Mary was told by the angel Gabriel that she would give birth to God's Son. The child's name was to be Jesus, and His birth would be miraculous. Jesus was not conceived by a man but by the Holy Spirit of God (Luke 1:26-38). And as soon as Mary was with child, she couldn't wait to run and tell her cousin Elisabeth the good news.

A child in his mother's womb felt great joy

Elisabeth was also carrying a child in her womb. His name was John, and he was six months along. When Mary entered Elisabeth's house, she hugged and kissed Elisabeth and said hello to her. And when John heard Mary greet Elisabeth his mother, he jumped for joy in her womb (Luke 1:39-44).

Children in their mother's womb felt intense rivalry

Genesis 25:22 says that the twins Jacob and Esau were engaged in a bruising struggle when they were in their mother Rebekah's womb. And Hosea 12:3 says during that violent conflict in the womb, Jacob grabbed hold of his brother Esau's heel.

Aren't they just a clump of cells?

There are people who will tell you that a child in the womb is just a lump of tissue incapable of living outside the womb. But he or she is not a meaningless blob. Psalm 139:13-16 says the child in the womb is God's handiwork. God is a loving Father who weaves together the baby's bones and sinews.

From the moment of conception God knows that child and knits the child together in the womb. God sees the child developing in the womb — the place He provided for their protection. That unborn child is a person in the fullest sense of the word.

Doesn't life "begin at breath"?

Genesis 2:7 says that Adam became a living person when God blew the breath of life into Adam's face. This leads some to conclude that because a child in the womb doesn't breathe air, they are therefore not a living being, and will not become one until they emerge from the womb at birth and take their first breath.

But the lesson from Genesis 2:7 is not that life begins when we breathe, but that life comes from God. Adam was an exception in that God created Adam from the dust of the earth. Adam was never in a womb (Genesis 2:7). Adam was the first man, and the wonderfully graphic description of God *breathing* into Adam's nostrils is symbolic of the fact that God gives life to every one of His living creations (Isaiah 42:5).

A child in the womb doesn't need to breathe air in order to be alive or to be a person. In Genesis 9:4 and Leviticus 17:11, God tells us that *the life of living beings is in their blood.*

In Genesis 9:5-6, God says that whoever commits murder must face the death penalty. God calls murder "the shedding of blood," and He says the murderer must pay with "the blood of their life," meaning death.

So a baby in his or her mother's womb
gets their life through the blood which flows through their veins
while they are in the womb.

The sacredness of a mother's womb

Over twenty times in the Old Testament the word "womb"
comes from the Hebrew word *rechem*. "*Rechem*" is # 7358 in
the Hebrew dictionary in *Strong's Concordance*. It comes
from the verb *racham*, which is # 7355. "*Racham*" means to
love, to show compassion, to have mercy. The womb is the
place where the newly formed child is loved, and shown
compassion and mercy.

How does God feel about people mistreating His gay child?

After taking my Bible Quiz, a young man told me he was gay, and in his country he could be killed if people found out. I wrote the following for him. I know, the people who need to hear this the most might not read it. But you never know what good could come if it changes one person's mind.

You know that verse in the Bible? It's the one people call the Golden Rule, which says: "Do unto others as you would have them do unto you — but not if they're gay." It's right there in the Book of First Pollutions. (Actually, there's no such verse in the Bible. My apologies to Matthew 7:12).

When it comes to people who call themselves gay, you are not their judge, jury, or executioner. And if you do act as though you are, then you've entered very dangerous territory, because now you're stepping on God's toes — and He doesn't like that. He will judge you for doing that. Some mistakenly think that if a person is gay then it's okay to be rude, insulting, and cruel to them, or to act in a way that makes them feel threatened. People justify violence by seeing their victim as an other, a less-than, by thinking of them as nonhuman. But before you go around behaving like that, you had better seriously consider the following:

 God created that person — they are His child

And you know how a parent reacts when somebody messes with their child, right? So, look out. God loves that person so much that He gave His only Son, Jesus, to go to the cross and die for that person (1 John 2:2). If you mistreat someone God loves *that* much, how do you think He will feel about *you*? He will be angry with you (James 3:8-10).

Always remember, God is the boss, not you.

What can I do if I'm being bullied?

When I heard about a young woman who was bullied and then took her own life, I wanted to write something and make it available at the Quiz. My street preacher friend Tilman told me: "Whatever it is, live with it and wait it out." I'm not saying you should take abuse. No, get help. But know that time goes by; you'll move on. And with God there is great hope and comfort. Proverbs 18:10 says that God is a strong tower, and you can choose to run into that tower and be safe. It means your soul is safe.

Life has challenges, and the Bible teaches us how to deal with them. First Corinthians 10:13 says there is no difficulty afflicting us that is not also being experienced by others. Please don't commit suicide. Don't murder God's precious child. There is another way. In the Holy Bible, God tells us that He is love. He knows what you're going through — you're His child. He created you and He loves you more than you could ever imagine or believe. You can trust God. (Psalm 34:17-18; Isaiah 26:3; 1 John 4:8)

Come to God as you are — no matter how messed up you might be. He already knows about it anyway. Come to Him humbly, broken and crushed, and He will welcome you. Don't act out. Don't ruin your life. You can get through this. I was punched and chased in grammar school and junior high. They pick on anyone who's different. A lot of times the kids who are different turn out to be really special adults. You can get through this with peace and joy in your heart, even when tears are streaming down your face. And God will use what you've been through — your suffering, and the unique person you've become because of it. You'll be a wiser, stronger person because you didn't let it defeat you. And you will have learned how to comfort others (2 Corinthians 1:3-4).

God will not allow you to be tried beyond what you are able to bear. God will provide a way out — if you ask Him (1 Corinthians 10:13). If you turn to Him, trust in Him, talk to Him in prayer. Earlier, I said, "There is a way." Jesus is the Way. And He has a family with members all over the world — a truly loving family waiting for you (Ephesians 2:19-22).

Let me tell you about Jesus, who He is. Jesus is God. Yes, the very God that created you and loves you. Being God, He is all-powerful, so He can do anything. He knows everything about you. Jesus will never disappoint you, never leave you, never forsake you. He will give you a peace that surpasses anyone's ability to comprehend (John 14:27; Hebrews 13:5).

> Jesus often said these words to people: "Fear not." (Matthew 14:27; Luke 12:32; Revelation 1:17). In the Bible, the prophets, apostles, and other believers went through trials many times. We can endure hardship with God right there with us, making His presence felt.

You can have the great pleasure of reading and studying the Bible, asking God for wisdom, and you'll grow in maturity. He will change you; *you'll see life in a totally new way* (2 Corinthians 5:17). And you'll have the pleasure of meeting your Christian brothers and sisters.

In Matthew 11:28-30, Jesus said:

"Come to Me,
all of you who toil and are burdened,
and I will give you rest.
Take My yoke upon you, and learn of Me;
for I am meek and lowly in heart:
and you shall find rest for your souls.
For My yoke is easy, and My burden is light."

To be yoked means to be joined together. Walk with God in your troubles. *He* will save you. He is a mighty fortress. He is the Rock. Run to Him.

God will take you under His wings, if you have Jesus Christ as your Lord and Savior, repenting of your sins, loving Him, obeying Him, following Him. Then you can claim the promises in the Bible. You have to ask (Psalm 18:2; 46:1; 91:4; Matthew 7:7-8).

Does feeling suicidal make me a bad person?

Whe you're in deep despair and you want your life to end, it's made worse by the feeling that you are the only one in the world who's going through it. Fortunately, the Bible gives an honest account of its heroes, and we see that they're just like us. Be comforted by that, and reassured. Our God is merciful, and He can do anything.

Are you like me? I know what it's like to be so low that I've screamed at God — "If You're going to treat me like this, then just go ahead and kill me!" You too? But do you know who else said those very same words to God? Moses did (Numbers 11:15). Why did Moses say that to God? Because he was human just like us.

 Despair, anger, and feelings of hopelessness are part of the human experience. You and I are not the only ones who go through those things (Acts 14:15; 1 Corinthians 10:13; James 5:17).

We know what it's like to feel alone and abandoned, as though no one knows we exist, and no one cares. It's surprising, though, that Moses would say "Kill me!" to God, because Moses had an advantage we can only dream of — the Bible tells us God spoke to Moses face to face, like a person speaks to their friend (Exodus 33:11).

What's my point? Other than Jesus, there's no one else in the Bible who had such an intimate relationship with God as Moses did. But despite that, Moses despaired of life just as we have. Moses led the children of Israel out of captivity in Egypt and through the wilderness for forty years, but God wouldn't let Moses enter the Promised Land because of a serious sin he committed. The great Moses was no better than us — he messed up too (Numbers 20:1-12). Still, when Moses died he was buried by God Himself, an honor given to no one else. And Moses was present with Elijah when Jesus displayed His glory on the Mount of Transfiguration (Deuteronomy 34:5-6; Matthew 17:1-3).

Other biblical heroes who wanted to die

Elijah the prophet obeyed God and boldly confronted the murderous king Ahab, defending God's glory against 850 false prophets. God did mighty things through Elijah, even bringing a dead boy back to life. Yet one time, in a moment of despair and hopelessness, Elijah told God he'd had enough and he asked God to take his life. But God made sure that Elijah knew he wasn't alone (1 Kings 17:21-22; 18:17-40; 19:1-4,18; 2 Kings 2:11).

Job cursed the day he was born, and asked God to kill him (Job 3:1-8; 6:8-9; 7:15-16; 10:1).

Jonah said it would be better to die than to live, and wished he would die (Jonah 4:8).

Jeremiah lacked the successes Moses and Elijah had. His life was filled with sorrow. He was so driven to the depths of despair, that he wished he'd never been born. Jeremiah was unsuccessful except for one thing — God spoke through Jeremiah about the Savior, the Lord Jesus Christ, our hope, God with us (Jeremiah 20:1-18; 33:14-16).

Feeling suicidal doesn't make you a bad person and it doesn't mean you're hopeless. It's been years since the last time I screamed at God to kill me. What changed? It took action on my part. Now I am giving my life to Jesus Christ. He is my Lord and Savior, friend and comforter. Life can get very difficult, and God understands. He knows what we're made of.

Our biggest problem is our disobedience to God

God expects us to turn to Him and obey Him, and that means suicide's not an option. *"Thou shalt not murder [oneself]"* (Exodus 20:13; Luke 6:46; 11:28).

Jesus is there in the Bible. Read the Proverbs, Psalms, Gospel of John. Get on your knees and talk to God. Believe in Him and one day He will dry your tears for good (Matthew 11:28-30; Revelation 21:3-7).

How can I forgive someone who hurt me?

Can't forgive? Do you know how God feels about that? He doesn't like it. Why? Because God is willing to forgive us for sinning against Him (1 John 1:9). It makes no sense for us to accept God's great mercy, and then turn around and be unwilling to forgive someone who did us wrong. Do we think we're better than God?

But they got away with it! I want everybody to know what they did. I want them brought to trial. I want to ask them why. I want them to pay. I want them to suffer! It's a private hell. Torment. Over and over in your mind and chest, pounding, torture. You can't stop. You don't want to stop. You want justice, maybe even revenge. And maybe they did apologize, maybe they were convicted and punished, they *did* suffer — but you're still in anguish.

You can use the teachings and the power found in the Bible to get yourself free. Then you'll win.

God said in His law that we are to love our neighbor as ourselves (Leviticus 19:18). But during the time of Jesus, the people changed God's law into their own version, which was, *Love your neighbor, but hate your enemy.*

God didn't say that, and Jesus told them so:

"Now you have your saying: Love your neighbor, but hate your enemy. Well, I have My saying: Those people who have an intense hatred toward you, who would love to do you harm — I want you to love those people.

"There are people who hate you so much that they come after you like lions chasing a rabbit. I'm telling you to pray for them.

"There are people who hate you so much they wish you
were dead, people who tell lies about you, and threaten and
intimidate you. I want you to speak well of those people.

"And if you make it your heart's desire to live by this saying
of Mine, then you'll be living like a child of God in heaven.

"Because God gives sunlight to good people *and* to evil people.
And God gives rain to those who love to do what's right *and*
to those who love to do what's wrong.

"Therefore, I want you to strive to be mature, to become
complete Christians, who love all people, like God does."

- Matthew 5:43-45,48

Jesus didn't just talk the talk, He showed us how it's done
How so? His closest friends were disloyal. The religious authorities
found people willing to tell lies about Him so they could have Him
executed. Jesus was mocked, punched, spit on, paraded through
the streets, and nailed to a cross to die. They did this to an innocent
man, the sinless Jesus (Matthew chapter 26; Mark chapter 15).

> Yet Jesus told God from the cross, that He wanted God to
> forgive them (Luke 23:34).

 Now here's where it gets serious. *God said that
if we refuse to forgive people for what they do to us,
then He won't forgive us for what we do to Him.
We are all guilty too — we've all hurt God's feelings —
but God is willing to forgive us (Matthew 5:7; 6:14-15; 18:23-35).

If you're still angry, please don't destroy yourself by disobeying
God. Declare war on those feelings by taking shelter in Jesus, the
faithful friend, forever (John 15:13-15). You have to fight those feelings
every day. Let God take you under His wing, and give you peace
of mind (Psalm 91:4; Romans 12:19-21).

How do I resist temptation?

The following is one of my favorite questions to use at the Quiz.

I'm thinking of two individuals, one in the New Testament and one in the Old. Each of them had a conversation with the devil. The devil tried to get them to do wrong by reasoning with them, asking questions, and making tempting offers.

The devil couldn't defeat the one in the New Testament. That one responded to the temptations by quoting Scripture, God's Word from the Bible (Luke 4:1-13). But the devil was able to defeat the one in the Old Testament because they didn't cling to what God said.

So, who are the two?

The one in the New Testament is Jesus. Right after Jesus was baptized, God's Holy Spirit took hold of Him. It was like when the Secret Service agents take hold of the president and rush him away. The Spirit took Jesus to the wilderness so the devil could try to get Jesus to do wrong — to commit sin by disobeying God. The devil presented Jesus with three temptations.

 Jesus used *the sword of the Word of God* to fight off each temptation by faithfully quoting God's Word, appropriately and accurately. And He used *the shield of faith* to snuff out all of the devil's enticements (Deuteronomy 6:13,16; 8:3; Ephesians 6:16-17).

The one in the Old Testament is Eve. She added to and took away from God's Word. No wonder the devil defeated her. In Genesis 3:1, the devil said to Eve, "Could God have possibly said you can't eat from every tree of the Garden?" That question was meant to introduce doubt into Eve's mind.

Eve replied, "We can eat the fruit from the trees in the Garden." But she took away from God's Word by omitting the word "freely." God said they can *freely* eat (Genesis 2:16; 3:2).

Then Eve told the devil, "Regarding the one tree, God said, 'You shall not eat from it, nor touch it, or you will die.'" Eve added to God's Word — God never said, "Don't touch it." And she took away from God's Word by removing the emphasis. What God said was, "You will *surely* die" (Genesis 2:17; 3:3).

The devil told Eve, "You will *not* surely die." That was a blatant lie. And the devil promised Eve that if she ate from the tree, her eyes would be opened and she would become like a god (Genesis 3:4,5; John 8:44).

> Eve chose to believe the devil instead of God.

The devil presented Eve with a threefold temptation. Genesis 3:6 says Eve saw that the tree was good for food, pleasant to look at, and desirable because it would make her wise. That corresponds with 1 John 2:16 (KJV): "All that is in the world, the lust of the flesh, and the lust of the eyes, and the pride of life, is not of the Father, but is of the world." Eve ate from the tree and gave to Adam, who also ate. As a result of this, death entered the Garden of Eden and spread to the world (Romans 5:12).

Eve was not able to resist temptation because she didn't stick to God's Word like Jesus did. That's why she was defeated.

> Jesus stayed with God's pure Word, showing us by His example that if we trust God, we can resist the devil's temptations (Ephesians 6:11-18; 1 Peter 2:2).

Why is it wrong to smoke weed?

Some say weed is harmless, and at first it might seem so. But have you asked God if He wants you to smoke weed? And have you studied what smoking weed does to your lungs and brain?

Popular culture makes things like weed, cigarettes, and drunkenness seem appealing. But it's a cruel trick, and falling for it will lead to misery. You might not realize it, but weed is a powerful drug. Weed can torture you with psychological addiction to the point where you won't be able to do anything without getting high first. People very often find themselves doing things to get weed that they'd never do otherwise. How many times have you bought weed for someone so you could pinch some for yourself? That person you bought weed for is God's child, and God will hold you accountable.

Are you using weed to find spiritual enlightenment?
God used the Greek root word *pharmakois* to describe those who provide a spell-giving potion, who use drugs to seek spiritual enlightenment. The word *pharmakois* means magicians, sorcerers — poisoners. God wants you to stop doing that and turn to Him for deliverance, or He will condemn you (Revelation 21:8).

You have troubles
Do you smoke weed to cope with life's troubles and pains? Well, how's this for troubles? What if you did nothing wrong but the authorities found people who were willing to tell lies about you? Then they used those lies to sentence you to death. You're arrested, whipped, slapped, mocked, punched, spit on, and humiliated by being made to carry a cross upon which you're nailed and raised up in the hot sun for all to see. As you writhe in pain, people yell insults at you. That's what happened to Jesus. Was it painful? The English word "excruciating" which is used to describe unbearable pain, comes from the Latin word for "crucifixion" (Matthew 26:59-61, 67; 27:26-31; Mark 15:29-32; Luke 23:13-15).

Jesus refused to be drugged

Before they nailed His wrists and feet to the cross and raised Him up to endure a slow, excruciating death, Jesus was shown one act of mercy. He was offered a drink laced with narcotics. But Jesus refused to drink it — knowing full well the pain He was about to experience (Matthew 27:34; Mark 15:23).

 One day you will have to face God and be judged
If Jesus refused narcotics when He was about to be tortured to death, then imagine how wrong it is to use weed or other drugs to get high or to party (Hebrews 9:27).

But you can repent, change your mind, right now. Fall to your knees, cry out to God, ask Him to forgive you, and He will. It will be like none of it ever happened. You'll have a clean record. And you won't even be held accountable for those you influenced. It will be over; you'll have peace of mind (Psalm 103:8-14; Isaiah 1:18; Romans 5:1; 1 John 1:9).

Strength will come from God through Bible study and prayer

God will give you what you need (Ephesians 6:10-18).

The apostle Paul wrote:

> I have the strength to do everything I need to do,
> because of the strength of Jesus Christ that is within me.
>
> - Philippians 4:13

Are you a Christian who smokes weed?

A Christian has the Holy Spirit living inside them, letting them know when they've committed a serious sin. If you don't feel the Holy Spirit telling you that God doesn't want you to smoke weed, then it's time for you to stop and take a serious look at your Christian walk (Hebrews 12:8).

What's the cure for racism?

There are Christians who claim the Bible says races should be kept separate. But the Bible teaches no such thing. People misuse the Bible to try and justify their own beliefs. Are you racist? Jesus can take that away and put love in your heart instead.

Can any of us say we've never had unkind feelings towards someone because of their race, nation, or culture? The question is, do we love those feelings or do we hate them? They are a sin in our hearts, where pride and deceit also reside (Mark 7:20-23).

God doesn't look at outward appearances. God looks at the heart (1 Samuel 16:7).

God blessed the apostle Peter's nation by giving them His law so they could learn how to be holy, and not take part in the wicked practices of other nations. But human nature is such that it went to their heads. For the sake of argument, I'm calling Peter's nation a race (Deuteronomy 7:1-7).

Racism is the belief that *they* are inferior to *us*. Peter's people saw those of other races, or other nations, as unclean and unworthy. There was even a ritual washing they would perform to cleanse themselves after they had been in public places (Mark 7:4; Acts 11:1-3).

But God didn't give His law to Peter's nation so they could keep it to themselves. God entrusted them with His law so they could bless the others nations of the world by teaching them what God requires (Isaiah 42:6-7; 49:6).

In Acts chapter 10, God taught the apostle Peter a lesson. Peter was staying with a man named Simon. One day, Peter went up to the roof of Simon's house to pray. It was lunchtime, and Peter started thinking about the food that was being prepared in the kitchen. But those thoughts suddenly vanished. Peter's mind was transported. He saw something spiritual, not of this world. It was God communicating with Peter supernaturally.

God showed Peter a sheet with animals on it. Some were animals that God permits us to eat, called clean, and some were animals God forbids us to eat, called unclean (Leviticus 11:1-47). The sheet was held up by its four corners, which meant that all the animals were forced into the middle and mixed together. Then Peter heard a voice say, "Rise Peter, kill and eat" (Acts 10:13).

Let me tell you the point of all this. *God wasn't telling Peter to eat unclean animals.* Right after Peter saw the sheet, he was asked to go to the house of a man named Cornelius — one of those whom Peter's people kept away from, the ones they called "unclean." But God knew that Cornelius was a good man (Acts 10:1-2).

When Peter met Cornelius, he said:

 "I'm sure you know that my people are forbidden to be
friends with, or even enter the house of, those of your race.
But God has shown me that I must never call any person unclean.
I truly understand now that God does not play favorites.
He accepts anyone who reverences Him and wants to do
what's right. Their race or nation has nothing to do with it."
- Acts 10:28, 34-35

So Peter shared the gospel of Jesus Christ with Cornelius and his family. They were all saved, received God's Holy Spirit, and were baptized (Acts 10:36-48). That was the lesson God taught Peter with the sheet.

Peter's racism was cured by his obedience to God

My loved one died. Where are they now?

One of the most common questions is: "I don't know if my loved one was saved — so how do I know if they went to heaven or hell?"

You've probably gotten the idea from popular culture that when some people die they go straight to hell. There's a problem with that — because *no one* is in hell right now. No one goes to hell until after the great final judgment.

So where are those who have died?
Ecclesiastes 12:7 says that when you die
your physical body becomes dust again,
and your spirit returns to the One who gave it to you.
 And that, of course, is God — you return to God.
 [If you *return* to God, that means you *came* from God.
 He created you] (Genesis 1:27; Luke 23:43).

Yes, everyone's spirit returns to God when they die. But the final judgment won't happen until *after* Jesus comes and rules as King of the earth for a thousand years (Revelation 20:1-15).

Take comfort in the knowledge that your loved one is with God. It's okay to pray for them if you wish. Just remember that God is the judge — so leave it in His hands.

... our body will go back to the dust of the earth
where it came from, and our spirit will return
to the One who gave it to us — God, our Creator.

- Ecclesiastes 12:7

Is my soul immortal?

No, your soul is not immortal. Your soul can die.

In Matthew 10:28, Jesus said:

> "You should not be afraid of those who kill the body but
> can't kill the soul. Rather, you should fear the One who
> is able to destroy both body and soul in hell."

The One who is able to destroy both body and soul in hell is God.

Romans 2:7 says that God will give eternal life to those who persevere through challenges and obstacles, and continue to do what's right. They are proving to God that their faith in Jesus is genuine, and they truly desire to live forever.

 You are not immortal.
God can destroy your soul or He can give you immortality.

God said there's only one way to have immortality, and that is by believing in the Lord Jesus Christ (John 3:16).

Chapter Ten

Money

Will you use up your whole life chasing after more and more money like a hawk hovering over its prey?

God's not impressed with your money. To Him it's nothing.

And before you can satisfy your desires, the money you spent your life hunting down will grow eagle's wings and fly away, disappearing into the clouds.

- Proverbs 23:5

Do Christians have to give 10%?

One day when I was six years old, my dad said he wanted to tell me something. I realize now why he acted like it was a big deal. It was so I'd always remember it. He sat me down and told me there was a town with one church that rang its bells every day. One day the bells rang as usual, but the people in the town couldn't hear them. This went on day after day. So the people brought gifts to the church thinking then they would hear the bells. But it didn't work. There was a little boy in that town. He had one toy, a ball, his only possession. The boy gave the ball to the church, and then he heard the bells. Everyone brought gifts. Why was the boy the only one who heard the bells?

Why did Abraham hear the bells?
The first person in the Bible who gave 10% to God was Abraham. Immediately after God gave Abraham victory over his enemies in war, Abraham was met by Melchizedek, the king of Salem, priest of the most high God. Melchizedek brought bread and wine, and he blessed Abraham. Then Abraham gave Melchizedek a tenth of all the spoils that his men had seized. What's meant by "spoils" is the loot — the items that the victor takes from an enemy they have defeated (Genesis 14:18-20).

In Hebrews 7:1-4, the apostle Paul reminded us about the time when Abraham gave Melchizedek a tenth of the spoils of war. The word Paul used for "spoils" is the Greek word *akrothinion*. It's #205 in the Greek dictionary in the back of the *Strong's Concordance*. Literally, it means the top of the heap. Abraham didn't just give Melchizedek any old tenth. Abraham gave the best, the cream off the top. And Jesus said that Abraham heard the bells (John 8:56).

Will I hear the bells if I give 10% of the best?
The Pharisees gave God 10% out of their best things. Nobody gave 10% like the Pharisees. If they picked a hundred mint leaves from their herb garden, they'd give ten leaves to the church.

But Jesus said to them, "Sure, you Pharisees count out ten leaves of every hundred you grow in your herb garden and give them to God, and that's all well and good. But despite all that — you are doomed. Your problem — and it's a huge problem — is that you're not doing the things that really matter, things like justice, mercy, and faithfulness" (Matthew 23:23). The Pharisees were not hearing the bells.

Why couldn't the Pharisees hear the bells?

If you're thinking you're all set because you give 10% of your income to your church, you might be mistaken. The Pharisees didn't hear the bells because they didn't want to. Despite their perfect record of giving, Jesus told them they were failing. Why? They gave God 10% for the wrong reason. They wanted everybody to see how holy they were (Matthew 23:5).

If you want to hear the bells you have to do more than give things to God. You need to surrender yourself to God, take God's Word into your heart, and do what it says (Luke 8:21). The Pharisees didn't want to do that. Ananais and Sapphira gave money to the church. But they gave for the wrong reason. The truth came out when they were exposed as lying to God (Acts 5:1-11).

Jesus wants more than your money

When Jesus called Matthew to be one of His twelve apostles, Jesus went to Matthew's house for a meal. Many people came to the meal to see Jesus and hear Him speak. But these were the kind of people the Pharisees called sinners and undesirables. The Pharisees chided the disciples of Jesus, asking them why Jesus would eat with such people. But Jesus heard the Pharisees ask that question, and He answered them Himself. Jesus told the Pharisees, "I didn't come to call the righteous. I came to call sinners to repentance. Now go and learn what this means: 'I desire compassion, not the giving of things'" (Matthew 9:9-13). Jesus was quoting Hosea 6:6.

That's what Jesus was talking about when He told those champions of 10% giving, the Pharisees, that they were lacking justice, compassion, and faithfulness (Matthew 23:23). The Pharisees took the easy way — they gave things.

The hard way, the better way, the important way, is the way of a Christian heart that aches for the unsaved, for the ones who are humbly seeking the truth. And now, in the Christian age, it doesn't matter if you give 10% or 50% or 1% of your things. What matters is that you feel love and compassion — God's love and compassion — and you act on it. You act on it by "eating with sinners" so you can teach them the Bible and share the gospel (1 Samuel 15:22; Amos 5:21-24; Micah 6:6-8). You don't have to give to a church — you can start your own ministry and give your time, money, and effort to that.

What percentage does Jesus want?

Jesus was asked which of God's commandments was the most important. Jesus answered that question by quoting Deuteronomy 6:4-5. Jesus said the most important of God's commandments is:

> "You are to love the Lord your God with all your heart
> and all your soul and all your mind and all your strength"
> (Mark 12:28-30). Jesus used the word "all" four times.
> And the word means exactly what it says — ALL
> (Deuteronomy 10:12-13).

Jesus said, "Anyone who does not take up their cross and follow Me is not good enough for Me" (Matthew 10:38), and "Whoever does not carry their cross and come after Me, cannot be My disciple" (Luke 14:27). Where did a person go when they took up a cross? Crucifixion. Death. That's the percentage Jesus wants. That's 100%. Somewhere in the world on any given day, Christians are losing their jobs and homes, being raped, tortured, and slaughtered, because they follow Christ. When you become a Christian, you're supposed to make it known that you follow Christ. We do this by teaching truths from the Bible and sharing the gospel. We do it knowing that it could cost us our lives.

Why a little boy?

In our story, the one who hears the bells is a child. Why a child? One day people were bringing little children to Jesus so He could bless them. But His disciples told them, "No! Don't be bothering Jesus with those kids." When Jesus saw His disciples doing that, it hurt His heart.

Jesus told His disciples:

> "No, you stop! Let the children come to Me and do not hold them back. The kingdom of heaven belongs to those who are like these children. And here's something you had better understand: anyone who does not receive the kingdom of God like a little child — will never enter into it."

When Jesus finished setting the disciples straight, He turned to the children. Jesus picked up each one, wrapped His arms around them, placed His holy hands on them, and blessed them (Mark 10:13-16).

Jesus spoke of children that way to teach us how we should relate to God — with complete trust, childlike abandon, and a desire to please. We're not in it to impress people or to get an advantage for ourselves. We give and do with a pure heart, only looking to do what pleases God.

The ball was all the little boy had. He gave everything. Now suppose you give 10% of your income to a church, and even though you're losing 10% you still have a good lifestyle, a comfortable life. But you did your duty, you're all set, right? The boy's gift of the ball was different because it cost him something. He gave up what he valued most. He was willing to part with an earthly love to receive a heavenly gift in return. He was sincere — he truly wanted to please God. It was more important to him to hear the bells than to keep his prized possession. The lesson for us is that we have to be willing to give everything and suffer anything for Jesus (Mark 10:28-30; Luke 14:26).

There was a woman who came to Jesus and broke a precious alabaster box of fragrant oil to anoint Him. That broken box was symbolic of her — she gave everything. Jesus said that in breaking the box she was showing much love to Him in gratitude for being forgiven for her sins (Luke 7:36-50). If you want to hear the bells, you have to give Jesus 100%. Jesus gave 100% for us (2 Corinthians 8:9).

What's the right attitude when giving to God?

God's children give because they love to hear God speak

In the Old Testament, God told Moses to build what was called the tabernacle. This was where God would come down from heaven to meet with His people on earth. And there were priests who acted on behalf of the people. That all changed after Jesus died and was resurrected. Now every Christian is a priest who doesn't need a man to go to God for them. The tabernacle symbolized Christ (Hebrews 9:11).

Moses needed materials to build the tabernacle. God gave orders to all those in the congregation who had wisely given their hearts to the Lord — all those who felt inclined to do good. The orders were that they should take their bronze, silver, gold, and other precious items and give them as a contribution to the Lord for the building of the tabernacle.

Every one of the people who had a willing heart and a generous spirit went home to get the items needed to build the tabernacle, and they brought them to Moses (Exodus 35:4-29).

Loyal women of God show how it's done

There was one group in the congregation that Moses singled out. This was a group of women who faithfully assembled together at the door of the tabernacle. The Hebrew word used to describe their assembling is a word used for those who fight in war. These women are said to have assembled in troops. Were they an elite force of devoted warriors in God's army? Moses chose to honor them by recording what they did. They had the privilege of donating the bronze that would be used to build the laver for the tabernacle.

The women saw Christ in the tabernacle

Before the priests could do their service, they had to wash in a huge tub made out of bronze. It was called a laver. This was one of the holiest items in the tabernacle. Washing in the laver was symbolic of being washed in the blood of Christ for salvation and then being cleansed by the living water of God's indwelling Holy Spirit — things that would happen 1,500 years later (Titus 3:5).

A gift symbolic of giving all to God

And do you know what these women gave up — what they gave to God so the bronze laver that represented salvation could be built? They gave up their mirrors, which are also called "lookingglasses" (KJV). At that time mirrors were made out of metal. Giving over their mirrors to God's service was a giving up of self for God's glory. It came from their hearts. The thought of getting rich because they gave would never have entered the minds of these good women. Theirs was a deliberate act meant to show they cared little for their own advancement, but rather would give all for God (Exodus 38:8).

They didn't want treasures on earth, but in heaven

Those mirrors would have been precious possessions to the women, made of the best bronze. But the thought of using them for themselves became as nothing to them. They wanted to show God that it was *Him* they loved, not their own selves. And they gave the mirrors for the good of their fellow believers, to have this holy place to hear from God.

They gave with a willing heart, a generous heart, a zeal to do their duty for God, like good soldiers for Christ. Mirrors are part of the vanity of this world. These loyal women showed God they cared little for the fleeting pleasures of the world. Their hearts were for the eternal. They wanted treasures in heaven, rather than on earth.

That was the lesson Jesus taught in Matthew 6:19-21 ...

Where do you want your heart to be? In the decaying things of this temporary world, or in heaven where there's no loss, and everything lasts forever?

Didn't Jesus tell Christians to sell their possessions?

Skeptics often ridicule Christians by asking, "Instead of being concerned with 'political issues,' why don't you do what Jesus told you to do — sell your possessions and help the poor?"

Did Jesus say those words?

A certain man came to Jesus and asked, "What must I do to have eternal life?" Jesus replied, "Sell your possessions and give to the poor."

But the answer to the question: *What must I do to have eternal life?* is — *follow Jesus.* Why didn't Jesus *just* say "Follow Me"? Instead, Jesus added, "Sell your possessions and give to the poor." And when the man heard that, he turned his back on Jesus and walked away. We're told that the man felt great sadness because he had many possessions. Jesus said "sell your possessions" to *that* man in order to reveal the man's heart. Jesus knew that man was not ready to follow Him with his whole heart (Matthew 19:16-22).

But didn't Jesus tell His disciples to sell their possessions?

Yes, Jesus did say to His disciples, "Sell your possessions and give to the poor" (Luke 12:33). But Jesus did *not* mean it literally. If a person sold all their possessions they would die of hunger and cold. When Jesus told the man who asked about eternal life to sell his possessions, that man took it literally. He believed Jesus actually wanted him to sell all he had. But selling one's possessions is *not* a requirement to become a disciple of Jesus. There were some among the disciples who had money — Joseph of Arimathaea, Joanna, and Susanna are named (Matthew 27:57; Luke 8:3).

What did Jesus really mean?

Jesus was intense. He would hit people right between the eyes with His direct, overstated, point-blank way of giving orders. He had to speak that way because of the seriousness of His warnings and to get through people's thick heads. When Jesus told the disciples to sell their possessions, He was speaking in the exaggerated way He often spoke. It's like when He said you can't follow Him if you don't hate your father and mother (Luke 14:26). Jesus doesn't want you to hate your parents. And He doesn't need you to prove your love for Him by selling everything you have and becoming homeless and naked. You can obey the commandment of Jesus to "sell your possessions" while having a job, a family, a house, a car, a shotgun, and all kinds of possessions.

 That's because *"sell your possessions" is a state of mind*. What Jesus means is He wants you to love Him so much that if loving Him *did* cost you everything you have, you'd be willing to give it all up. Unlike the man who chose his possessions over Jesus, you would choose Jesus over your possessions (Luke 14:33).

A false gospel
The true way of salvation through Jesus Christ is called the "gospel," which means good news. There are many, though, who proclaim a false gospel. The Bible says that everyone who proclaims a false gospel is doomed (Galatians 1:8-9). One false gospel is the sell-your-possessions-and-give-to-the-poor gospel. It was created by wolves in sheep's clothing, so-called Christians, by removing the true meaning of certain Bible passages and giving those passages a different meaning, which they use to mislead people who don't know the true gospel.

I want to show you a trick
There's a trick used by the people who peddle the sell-your-possessions gospel to fool you into thinking Christians are supposed to devote their lives to helping the poor. They cite Luke 4:18, which says that Jesus came to proclaim the gospel to the poor. But in this verse "the poor" doesn't mean those who lack money. Luke 4:18 is a quote from the Old Testament, from Isaiah 61:1, which says Jesus came to proclaim the gospel to "the meek." Jesus doesn't look at outward circumstances. He doesn't prefer poor people over rich. Jesus looks at the heart.

Jesus wants meek, humble people — rich and poor — who are willing to give Him their whole heart and obey Him (1 Samuel 16:7).

Didn't Jesus enforce a lifestyle of poverty on His disciples?

When Jesus sent His disciples off to proclaim the gospel, He told them not to bring money with them on their trip, and not to bring a change of clothes or extra sandals, not even a walking stick. Sounds pretty rough, right? But look at what Jesus said straight after that, the reason He gave for sending them off without provisions: "The worker deserves to be fed." Jesus was sending them to the lost sheep of the nation of Israel, who knew God would bless those who provided food, clothing, shelter, and other aid to the teachers of His Word (Deuteronomy 25:4; Matthew 10:9-10).

What *did* Jesus tell Christians to do?

If Jesus commanded Christians to devote themselves to helping the poor, then His apostles and the early church disobeyed Him. Although they *did* help fellow Christians who were in need, we read nothing about them taking up a war on poverty. They didn't work at soup kitchens, and they didn't demand that the government fund more social programs.

> The work that Jesus *did* give Christians to do is the teaching of the gospel, the real gospel, the true way of salvation. The real gospel is the commandment of Jesus to all people to turn from sin and trust in Him.

Anybody can help the poor. But only Christians can give people the gospel of Jesus Christ, which saves souls from hell and gives eternal life (Matthew 4:17; 28:19-20, John 6:28-29). That's what Jesus wants Christians to "give to the poor," meaning the humble, whether rich or poor.

Why are Christians always asking for money?

Have you seen Christians on TV blubbering that they'll have to go off the air if people don't send them money? I say, "Good, go off the air. God never wanted you on the air in the first place." But they say they need the money to share the gospel. Then I say, "Great. Get yourself a pen and paper, make a sign inviting people to talk to you about the gospel, and go stand on a street corner. Then you can stop begging for money and making Christianity look bad."

Christians or con men?

The Christians you see on TV asking for money aren't Christians. They're con men (and women). All they're doing is using Christianity as a way to get your money so they can fatten themselves.

Why do some Christians talk about money all the time?

In Matthew 12:34, Jesus said that whatever delights a person's heart will overflow their heart and come out of their mouth in the words they speak. Your heart is you, the kind of person you are, what matters to you, what you love. If someone talks about money all the time, then that's what drives them. That's not Christianity. It's greed, which the Bible says is idolatry (Colossians 3:5). The apostle Paul wrote that the love of money causes people to do all kinds of evil things (1 Timothy 6:10).

Jesus warned that you can either give your heart, mind, love and obedience to money or to God. And if you choose money then you will hate God (Matthew 6:24). The apostle John wrote that those who choose to love the things of the world do not have a love of God in them (1 John 2:15).

Doesn't the Bible say preachers are to be paid?

Yes, the Bible teaches us to support those who teach us the Bible (Deuteronomy 25:4; Luke 10:7; 1 Corinthians 9:9-11; Galatians 6:6; 1 Timothy 5:17-18). But we don't support those who teach us the Bible so they can live a life of luxury. Jesus and the apostles didn't — they lived a simple, humble existence. And it doesn't mean Bible teachers are supposed to *ask* for money. You don't see Jesus or the apostles asking the believers to feather their nests. Jesus and the apostles didn't take — they gave. They had a tender, parental, self-sacrificial love for the believers.

If anyone deserved a salary it was the apostle Paul

No one went out and shared the gospel as much as the apostle Paul. And Paul's the one God chose to explain the gospel in detail in the many epistles (letters) which he wrote and which make up a sizable portion of the New Testament. If anyone was ever worthy to receive financial support, it was the apostle Paul. But Paul refused to accept a salary. He didn't want to take the chance that his receiving a salary could offend or confuse someone. Paul did not want to do anything that could hinder the sharing of the gospel of Christ (1 Corinthians 9:12). Some people might have been turned off if they knew Paul got paid. So instead of taking money from the believers, Paul supported himself by working as a tentmaker (Acts 18:3; 20:34). Paul said Christians are to be satisfied and happy if we have the basic necessities such as food and clothing (1 Timothy 6:8).

It's more blessed to give than to receive

Paul told the believers that he never lusted after their gold, silver, or clothing. Paul never wanted their money. The great apostle Paul turned down the support he deserved and had every right to. Instead he toiled away at manual labor to support not only himself but fellow Christians also. Paul said he always showed the believers by his example that it's our duty to work hard, so we can share what we gain with others (Acts 20:33-34; 2 Thessalonians 3:8-9). So, instead of spending their time begging for money, those "Christian" con men should get a job washing dishes and go after work to share the gospel. Paul told us that Jesus said, "It's more blessed to give than to receive" (Acts 20:35).

Because Paul led the believers to Christ by teaching them the gospel, Paul saw them as his spiritual children. In 2 Corinthians 12:14-15, Paul said he wouldn't take from the believers but rather, he would spend what he had for them.

Paul made his point by saying the parents lay up an inheritance for the children — the children don't lay up an inheritance for the parents.

The "Christian" con men pervert the truth

Con men take verses out of context and give them the wrong meaning. One of their favorite verses to misuse is Deuteronomy 8:18 which says: "God gives the power to get wealth." They put these words on coins and make them their words to live by. They do that to mislead people into thinking that God is a way to get rich. They indoctrinate people in the mindset that it's all about money, material pleasures, living a voluptuous life. And of course they tell you the first thing you have to do to get rich is give *them* money.

God is not a magic genie who grants your material wishes.

What God is really saying is that if you get wealth, remember that *He* is the one who gives you that wealth. It is a warning to His people that they must never forget that all blessings come from *Him*.

God doesn't want us to become proud and forget Him when we prosper in this world. He's warning us to humble ourselves and be thankful to Him (Deuteronomy 8:10-14).

They use Jesus to make money

In Matthew 24:4-5, Jesus warned us to beware of the many deceivers who will come in His name. The word "in," as in "in His name," is the Greek word *epi*. One scholar says that in this passage *epi* means "trading upon." So, Jesus is warning that many deceivers will come trading upon His name. In other words — making money off Him. They're deceiving you, using you to get rich.

Where did the idea of giving money to churches originate?

In the Old Testament, God told the children of Israel to give. The main purpose of the money given was to support the priests so they could work full-time serving God and teaching God's Word to the people (Leviticus 10:11; Numbers 18:20-21; Deuteronomy 31:9-13).

In the nation of Israel the church was the government. When the children of Israel gave money, it was like paying taxes. In addition to support for the priests, the money was also used for special events and as a way to help the needy (Deuteronomy 14:22-29).

In the New Testament the same principle applies

Christians should give to those who teach the Bible but we are not under obligation to give 10% like Israel was. If you are fortunate enough to find a good Bible teacher then do as you feel led. The first believers didn't give 10%. The apostles didn't tell them to give 10%. They gave spontaneously, cheerfully, out of compassion for the needs of their fellow Christians (Acts 2:45; 4:34; 2 Corinthians 9:7; 1 John 3:17).

What about helping the needy? We can do that when an opportunity presents itself, like the Samaritan did. But now we pay taxes to a government that provides many social programs to help needy people (Luke 10:25-37; Romans 12:13; 13:6-7; Galatians 6:10; 1 Peter 4:9).

So should I just give money to the church next door?

No! Don't do that. Do you know what they believe, what they teach? But they say they're a Christian church. Oh sure, they *say* that. Do you know how many churches call themselves Christian but teach their own beliefs instead of God's teachings from the Bible?

The fervent apostle John sounded the alarm with an urgent warning: God wants eagle-eyed Christians. Why? Because there are many who set themselves up as Bible teachers, but have departed from the true teachings given by Jesus Christ. If you support false teachers, then God considers you to be a partaker in the evil they are doing (2 John 1:9-11).

Should Bible teachers ask for money?

If someone feels led to give money to a Bible teacher, great. The Bible teacher should receive it. But *asking* for money? No way, that's crass. Jesus told the apostles, "I gave to you and didn't ask you to pay Me. Now, go and give to the people without asking them to pay you" (Matthew 10:8).

The apostle Peter warned us about people who become Bible teachers because of their lust for money. Peter said they want to trick you and use you, so they make up false teachings and tell you it's the Word of God. When Peter said they "use" you, he chose the Greek word *emporeuomai*. Yes, it sounds like the English word emporium, a place of business. That's the point. For these so-called Bible teachers who keep begging for money, it's a business, and they just see you as a way to make money. Peter said they "make merchandise of you" (2 Peter 2:3).

Going after money is the wrong way. The Bible says it's like chasing after something that's not real, and it will harden your heart towards God's Word (Mark 4:19). Paul wrote that people who want to get rich will fall into temptation. They get caught in a trap that robs them of God's blessings. Their burning greed makes them want one stupid thing after another — things that are bad for them, until they fall headfirst into ruin and condemnation (1 Timothy 6:9). Jesus taught that rather than being greedy, we should seek God and trust Him for our needs — warning us that where our treasure is, our heart will be there also (Luke 12:13-34).

What's the right attitude for Bible teachers?

Paul told the believers he never conned them, he never used pleasant words or flattery as a way to get their money (1 Thessalonians 2:5). If a Bible teacher tells you he needs your money to buy a jet so he can preach the gospel, then you've met a fake. There are no rock star Christians. If you hear Bible teachers saying God wants them to be rich, you're listening to fakes. Jesus doesn't want ego cases among His disciples. So He said something to bring us down to earth:

> "My disciples, when you do all the things I order you,
> then say, *'We are dispensable, menial workers.*
> *We've only done that which is owed by us.'"*   - Luke 17:10

Contentment
Paul said some people pretend to respect God as a way to make money, but real riches is to respect God and be contented (1 Timothy 6:5-6). Jesus said:

> "Don't lose sleep worrying about where your next meal will come from or what you'll wear ... God knows you need those things. Save your energy for the one most important thing. What's that? Seeking the kingdom of God. Make that your chief concern, and then God will give you everything you need."
> - Matthew 6:31-33

Poor Christians are rich because they're content
My friend Tilman the street preacher used to say, "If you have two cents, make that do." The apostle Paul said that because he had Jesus Christ he had learned to be content in any situation whether he had little or much (Philippians 4:11-13).

The prayer of Agur
Tilman showed me a passage in the Bible that I never forgot. It's the prayer of a man named Agur:

> Lord, I ask You two things for my life — please don't keep them from me. First, keep far away from me those things that are false and useless. And secondly, give me neither poverty nor riches. Just give me the food I need to maintain my health.

> Because if I become rich I might think I don't need You, and say, "Who is the Lord?" And if I fall into poverty I might be tempted to turn to crime and steal, and then I would dishonor You, my Lord.
> - Proverbs 30:7-9

Doesn't that Bible say that if you give, you will receive?

Yes, passages like Malachi 3:10 and Luke 6:38 say that if you give, then you'll receive. The more you give, the more you'll receive. You can get so much you'll be overflowing.

Bring offerings of all your goods into the treasury, so there will be food for those who serve in My house of worship. I, the Lord of heaven's armies, say, put Me to the test, prove Me right in what I promise you. If you obey Me and give as I say, then I will open up the windows of heaven. And I will pour out a blessing so big you won't have enough room to put it all.

- Malachi 3:10

"If you give, then you will receive. Imagine a shopkeeper filling a container for you, his customer. He wants you to get your full money's worth. So he fills the container with the best he has. He shakes it so it settles and he can add more. He presses it down so even more can be added. He gets so carried away in his zeal to satisfy you that when he hands the container to you, there's so much you have to sit down and it overflows into your lap. As you give, so shall you get."

- Jesus, Luke 6:38

But, get what? Money? Maybe. What I want from God is something better than money. I want the true riches: more understanding of the Bible; the blessings of good Christian fellowship; I want God to continue my Christian walk — to direct my feet, give me new callings, and help me to get the things I need to serve Him.

Get wisdom. Proverbs 4:7 says wisdom is the most valuable thing there is — so valuable that it would be worth trading everything you have to get wisdom. The best thing you can give people is wisdom, and the best thing you can receive is wisdom, from God. That's the true riches.

Wisdom speaks in the Book of Proverbs and says:

Choose my instruction instead of silver,
and my knowledge rather than the purest gold,
because wisdom is better than any earthly treasure.
And of all the pleasures that a person desires,
not one can be compared to wisdom.

I love those who love me,
and those who thirst for me will find me.
Riches and greatness are with me,
yes, never-ending riches and justice.
The fruit I produce is better than the best gold,
and my benefits are more valuable than the finest silver.

Oh the happiness of all those who obey my words!
They never quit, they stand at my gates watching for me,
and wait at my door for me, day after day.
Because whoever finds me finds the fountain of life
that flows from God. And God will make them acceptable to Him.
But those who fail to seek me are hurting themselves.
And all those who hate me love death.

- Proverbs 8:10-11,17-19, 34-36

If I have enough faith, will God make me rich?

One of the favorite traps used by "Christian" con men is the get-rich-by-seed-planting scam. They bait the hook and wait for suckers to bite. They say, "Prove you have faith in God by sending me money to 'preach the gospel.'" They promise that if you send them money, God will reward your faith — you'll get a check in the mail, or a high paying job, or maybe money will fall out of the sky. They terrorize their victims, warning them, "If you don't send me money, then you're sinning, you're disobeying God." And they scold their prey, saying, "If you don't live in a big house and drive an expensive car like I do, it's because you lack faith and you have not planted enough money as a seed into my ministry."

What is the real evidence of faith?
Think about the Christians who live in countries where they are persecuted. They lose their jobs, their possessions, and their lives. Those Christians don't suffer that way because they lack faith.

 Persecuted Christians are the ones with the most faith (Revelation 2:9-10).

Hebrews 11:35-38 gives us examples of people who had great faith. They were the salt of the earth, but the world saw them as evil and tormented them, oppressed, and persecuted them, treated them horribly. They were tortured, mocked, whipped, and imprisoned. They were homeless and had to use animal skins for covering. Some were stoned to death or stabbed to death. Some were even sawed in two. They had to hide in the desert, in mountains, in caves, and even in holes in the ground.

They didn't have to suffer that way. They could have chosen to deny God. But they didn't do that. They stayed faithful to God because they looked forward to being resurrected by Jesus Christ and enjoying eternal pleasures in heaven. That's faith. That's the evidence of great faith, not living in a big house or owning an expensive car.

Did Jesus lack faith?

According to the money-loving "Christian" con men, the more you have the "special, wealth-unlocking faith," the more money God's going to give you. But when a man came and told Jesus he would follow Him wherever He went, Jesus said, "I don't even have a home to lay down My head at night." Jesus stopped the man in his tracks and let him know you don't follow Jesus to get material comforts and luxuries. If you follow Jesus, then you had better know ahead of time that things are going to get rough (Luke 9:57-58; 2 Timothy 3:12).

You don't come to Jesus to get *things*. You come to Jesus when your heart has been struck through with the realization that your sinfulness will bring the wrath of God on you. Jesus knew homelessness, and He knew poverty. Jesus left heaven and humbled Himself to the point where He had to accept help from some of the women who followed Him (Luke 8:3). The "Christian" con men live in multimillion dollar houses and drive cars that cost hundreds of thousands of dollars. Do they think they have more faith than Jesus?

Did the apostle Paul lack faith?

Paul wrote to the believers and told them what he was going through. Paul said he was being pushed and shoved so much that he had to move from place to place and had no permanent home, and not even proper clothing. Paul spent nights tossing and turning from hunger and cold (1 Corinthians 4:11; 2 Corinthians 6:5; 11:27). Was this because Paul was lazy, or a poor worker, or lacked faith? No, Paul worked his fingers to the bone. Paul suffered those things because of all the persecution directed at him.

Did the apostle Peter lack faith?

Peter told a crippled man begging at the temple that he had no silver or gold, meaning he had no money. Peter was one of the main apostles, yet his pockets were empty. But what did Peter have? Faith! He told the crippled man: "In the name of Jesus Christ of Nazareth, get up and walk." As he took the man by the hand, the crippled limbs were instantly healed. The man got to his feet, started walking, leaping for joy, and praising God (Acts 3:6-8).

The Bible says whatever you ask for, you'll get. I asked for a Cadillac. Why didn't I get it?

> The person who asked me that question might have read what Jesus said in Matthew 7:7 — "Ask, and it will be given to you." But a few verses later, Jesus said that you have to be kind and merciful to other people (Matthew 7:12).
>
> In Mark 11:24, Jesus said if you want to have all the things you desire, then pray, believing that you will have them. But in the next verse, Jesus said, "And when you pray — forgive everyone you have anything against."

Why doesn't God give people whatever they ask for, like a Cadillac, or lots of money, or anything else they want?

Maybe they're not being kind or forgiving to others. Or it could be because of what God said in James 4:3, "You ask and don't receive because your motives are wrong." What God means is they're asking Him for something just to satisfy their selfish desires.

Jesus said He will give a person anything they ask for. But Jesus made it clear that His promise is limited to those who are His disciples, who only ask for things they will use to honor God (John 14:13).

 In Matthew 6:33, Jesus said that *before we do anything else we must seek God*, and strive to live our lives according to His standards. And *then* God will give us everything we need.

Psalms 37:4-5 says if we delight ourselves in the Lord, He will give us the wishes of our heart. That means the Lord will give our hearts the desires *He* wants us to have — the ones which will serve His purposes and long-range plans for us. And if we commit our life to Him and trust in Him, then He will make the things we desire come true.

Chapter Eleven

It's not what you've been told

In Matthew 24:4, Jesus gave us what might be His most important warning:

He said we must develop the ability to look deeply into things so that no one will be able to deceive us or lead us astray.

Are there three Abrahamic faiths?

People often refer to "the three Abrahamic faiths" of Judaism, Christianity, and Islam. But there are *not* three Abrahamic faiths. There is only one.

The name Abraham means "father of many nations" and yes, different nations were descended from Abraham. But if we're talking about "faiths," meaning religious beliefs, then Abraham is the father *only* of those individuals in each nation who put their trust in Jesus Christ for their salvation (Romans 4:1-3, 9-25).

> When Abraham believed what God said to him, it meant God could make Abraham righteous — worthy to be in heaven — by clothing Abraham with the righteousness made available by the sacrifice of Jesus Christ.
> Understand then that the children of Abraham are those who put their trust in what God did through Jesus Christ, as Abraham did.
> God showed Abraham what was to come — the gospel, the good news, meaning the death and resurrection of Jesus Christ. And when God said all the nations would be blessed through Abraham, God meant only those of each nation who put their trust in Christ for salvation.
> So then, all those who put their trust in Christ are blessed, along with Abraham, the man who believed God.
>
> - Galatians 3:6-9

"Abraham rejoiced to see My day: and he saw it, and was glad."

- Jesus, John 8:56 (KJV)

 If your religion does not believe in Jesus Christ as the only Lord and Savior, then your religion is not an Abrahamic faith (Genesis 12:1-4; 15:1-6; 17:1-7; 22:8; Galatians 4:22-31).

Did black people come from Noah's curse?

A distraught young black woman came to me at the Quiz and said she'd been told that black people were under a curse. She was grateful and relieved when I explained to her how she'd been lied to. Imagine someone saying that to a child. They're lucky they can't be arrested on charges of spiritual fraud.

In Genesis 9:20-27, Noah drank some wine and fell asleep. What I think happened next was Noah's son Ham saw that as an opportunity to lay with Noah's wife.

Here's why I think that: we're told that Ham "saw the nakedness of Noah" (Genesis 9:22). And Leviticus 20:17 uses the expression "see the nakedness of" as a delicate way of saying "have sexual relations." *Who did Ham have sexual relations with?* Genesis 9:21 says Noah was "uncovered" in his tent, and Leviticus 20:11 says if a man lies with his father's wife, he has uncovered his father's nakedness.

When Noah found out what his son Ham did, Noah cursed Canaan (Genesis 9:24-25) Who's Canaan? He's Ham's son. Is it possible that Canaan is the son who would be born from Ham sleeping with Noah's wife? When Noah cursed Canaan, he cursed Canaan's descendants to be slaves. The name Ham means "black." So some say that was how the "black race" began, and that "black" skin is a curse.

 But Noah's curse on Canaan has nothing to do with black people. Black people are *not* cursed. They are God's creation, His precious children, and He loves them just the same as He loves everyone else.

That so-called "curse of Noah" teaching is an evil, racist invention. Those who teach it are wrenching the meaning out of an incident in the Bible and forcing things into it that aren't there.

Does the Bible forbid interracial marriage?

No, the Bible does *not* forbid interracial marriage. Racists try to say it does by misusing verses such as Leviticus 19:19 which says, "don't plant different kinds of seeds in the same field." That has nothing to do with interracial marriage.

 When God told the nation of Israel not to marry foreigners, it wasn't about race. *It was because foreigners worshipped false gods* (Deuteronomy 7:2-6).

> The Lord said:
>
> If you marry foreigners,
> they will turn your children away from following Me,
> and they will worship the foreigners' gods instead.
>
> - Deuteronomy 7:4

Even the wisest man who ever lived, king Solomon, a pious man who built the Temple to the one true God in Jerusalem, was influenced by his foreign wives to worship their gods. And because of Solomon's unfaithfulness, God took the kingdom away from Solomon's son (1 Kings 11:1-12).

> Rahab wasn't an Israelite — she was of a Canaanite race — but she accepted the one true God, married an Israelite, and became part of the family tree of Jesus (Joshua 2:11; Matthew 1:5; Hebrews 11:31; James 2:25).

Did Jephthah burn his daughter?

I was horrified by what I heard being taught at a Bible study. They were going through Judges chapter 11, and the leader of the Bible study was telling the others that Jephthah burned his daughter as a sacrifice to God. He pointed to Judges 11:39 and said, "See, it says Jephthah fulfilled his vow and burned his daughter." At this point I'm thinking, *What should I do? I'm not a member of this church. Should I say something? Can I let these people think Jephthah burned his daughter?* Finally, I spoke up and said, "It doesn't say in Judges 11:39 that Jephthah burned his daughter. It says he fulfilled his vow, and she knew no man." After going back and forth about it for a while the leader said, "That's what this church teaches. You can take it up with them."

In Judges 11:30-31, Jephthah asked God to help him defeat Israel's enemies. Jephthah promised God that if he was victorious in battle, then upon returning home whatever he saw first he would devote to the Lord OR offer up as a burnt offering to God. Does your Bible say AND instead of OR? If it does, then it's wrong.

 What Jephthah saw first was his daughter. When Judges 11:39 says that Jephthah fulfilled his vow, it does *not* mean that Jephthah sacrificed his daughter as a burnt offering. *He devoted her to a life of celibacy to serve the Lord.*

That's why it says she "knew no man," meaning that she would never get married, and why verse 38 says that Jephthah gave his daughter permission to lament her virginity for two months with her friends. Verse 39 tells us: "Jephthah did with his daughter according to the vow which he vowed: and she knew no man."

There is *nothing* anywhere in the Bible that would lead us to believe that Jephthah burned his daughter. Quite the contrary. God hates child sacrifice and Jephthah is honored in Hebrews 11:32 as a man of great faith (Deuteronomy 12:31; Judges 11:37-40; Ezekiel 20:26; Matthew 19:12).

Hasn't the law been done away with?

I meet people at the Quiz who say it's okay for them to practice their sin because "the law's been done away with." When I ask them if that means it's okay to be a thief or a murderer, they respond with blank stares and silence.

I went to one of those local Bible studies held in people's homes. During the conversation I said, "The law is good," and gave Deuteronomy 22:8 as an example. It says you must put a railing around the roof of a tall building so people won't fall off. One man, a member of the church that sponsored the Bible study, said, "If people started falling off the roof, then I'd put up a railing."

That man was taught that God is *horrified* at the thought of people obeying the law, so he would have to wait until someone fell to their death and *then* put up a railing. It's sad what churches do to people. I wrote to that man's pastor. His response was, "See Romans 10:4," which says, "For Christ is the end of the law for righteousness to every one who believeth" (KJV).

His pastor thinks the word "righteousness" only means doing what's right. He tells his people that Romans 10:4 means Christ is the end of (did away with) doing things right in obedience to the law. He's wrong. Romans 10:4 is talking about when God examines a person in His court of law and finds them not guilty because they are in a state of righteousness.

Before Christ died on the cross for our sins, the only way a person could be found not guilty was by obeying the law perfectly. But no one can do that. So who does God find not guilty? Anyone who believes and trusts in Christ's righteousness (Romans 3:20-22).

Hebrews 8:13 does speak of something that's growing old, becoming obsolete, and about to disappear. But it's not talking about the law; it's talking about the old covenant, also know as the covenant of Moses, that old way of trying to possess righteousness by obeying the law. That's what is being done away with, because Jesus made a new covenant, a better covenant, with His body and His blood (Jeremiah 31:31-34; Matthew 26:26-28; Galatians 3:11; Hebrews 13:20).

Do you know why Jesus died on a cross? He did it to save us from our sins. Do you know what sin is? Sin is the breaking of God's law (1 John 3:4).

> If the law *was* done away with, then there would be no sin, and we wouldn't need to repent. We wouldn't need a Savior; Jesus would have died for nothing. So, we could eat, drink, and be merry, because we're all going to heaven — along with murderers, rapists, and thieves, right? Wrong.

You can say the law of gravity's been done away with, but you'll still suffer the consequences if you fall off a roof (Luke 11:28; Romans 3:31; 6:1; Ephesians 2:10).

 But doesn't the Bible say we're not under law, but under grace? Yes, and what's meant by "under" is "under the power of." *Christians are free from the power of the law to condemn us* because we can confess our sins to God in the name of Jesus, and be washed clean. We're "under the power" of God's grace and the righteousness of Christ (Romans 6:14-16; Galatians 3:13).

God's law is good. David said so, Paul said it, and Jesus did too. I love it when I find someone's wallet on the street and get an opportunity to obey Deuteronomy 22:1-3. God's law has always existed and always will. And God wants obedience now just as much as He ever did (Psalm 119:1-21; Ecclesiastes 12:13; Matthew 5:17-19; Romans 7:12; 1 John 5:3).

"If you love Me, keep My commandments." - **Jesus**, John 14:15

Does the Bible say women must be silent?

On more than one occasion, someone asked me what the Bible says about a practice they were engaging in. And I would tell them the Bible says that what they're doing is a sin. Then they would say, "Why should I have to stop doing what I want? The Bible says women aren't supposed to speak."

What they mean is:
"The Bible is ridiculous, so why should I have to obey it?"

The Bible isn't ridiculous. God is the author of the Bible, and He always makes sense. We must study His words carefully and apply them in context. Your Bible says something like:

> Women should be <u>silent</u> during the church meetings. It's not proper for them to <u>speak</u>. Instead, they are to put themselves under submissive obedience, as the law commands. But if they want to be taught a certain thing, let them ask their husbands at home. It is impolite for a woman to speak in church.

> - 1 Corinthians 14:34-35
> (written by God through the apostle Paul)

The word translated "<u>silent</u>" is the Greek word *sigao*. Paul uses the same word *sigao* in verse 28, where he tells people who speak foreign languages to be silent if no interpreter is available. And Paul uses *sigao* again in verse 30, where he says that if someone is talking during the Bible study, and someone else would like to make a point, then the one who's talking should "hold their peace" and let the other person make their point.

None of this is meant to insult or demean anyone. *It doesn't mean those people are never to speak.* It's about maintaining order in the meeting.

When Paul says it's not proper for the women to speak, the word "speak" is the Greek word *laleo*. In the context of this chapter, the word *laleo* means "chatter." There were women causing disorder in the church meetings by having side conversations during the Bible study.

 The subject of this chapter is correcting disorder in the church meetings.

These were married women. A wife is to honor God by her gracious deference to her husband. If she has a question about what's being taught at church, she is to honor her husband by waiting until they get home to discuss it with him. It would be indecorous if she didn't wait to ask him at home, and instead asked him during the meeting, or asked men other than her husband about it. This is about being obedient to the orderly arrangements that God has commanded us to follow in His law. God blesses those who obey Him (Luke 11:28; 1 Corinthians 11:3).

It's a lie to portray God as hating women, or to say that He wants women to be treated like imbeciles or animals. Those who do that just want to ridicule God as an excuse to stay in their sin.

Of course women are to speak. The Scripture says to everyone, both male and female:

> *If anyone declares with their mouth that Jesus is Lord, and believes in their heart that God raised Him from the dead, they will be saved. Because it is by believing in your heart that you are made right with God, and it is by confessing with your mouth that you are saved.*
>
> - Romans 10:9-10

Did Peter eat pork?

Didn't Paul rebuke Peter for pretending he didn't eat pork? Paul *did* confront Peter for acting dishonestly, but defining the gospel was on the table, not pork.

Peter never ate pork and Paul never ate pork. They obeyed God's laws that prohibit eating pigs and certain other animals (Leviticus 11:1-47).

Paul explained in Galatians 2:14 that the reason he confronted Peter was because Peter walked away from the truth of the gospel. When we say "the gospel," we're talking about how a person is saved. There's only one gospel — the Lord Jesus Christ died for our sins, was buried, and rose from the dead. We're saved by believing the gospel and putting our trust, our faith, in Jesus.
(Acts 16:31; 1 Corinthians 15:1-4; Ephesians 2:8-9)

What did happen with Peter and Paul?
Well, Peter was in the city of Antioch having regular fellowship with (eating with) new Christians called Gentiles, who were not circumcised in the flesh and had been saved by faith alone. But one day some men came from Jerusalem, which was a sort of headquarters for Christian leaders. They taught that a person *can't* be saved by faith alone — that before a person can be saved they must first be circumcised in the flesh and obey the law of Moses (Acts 15:1, 5-11; Galatians 2:12).

The men from Jerusalem didn't like the idea that people could join their elite club only by believing in Jesus. Peter feared becoming an object of scorn to these men for having fellowship with Christians who were not circumcised in the flesh. So Peter walked away and pretended he didn't know the Christians who were saved by faith alone (Acts 11:1-3; Galatians 2:12).

That's why Paul stood in Peter's way and put up a fight, man to man. Peter was doing harm to those true Christians who were saved by faith. And Peter was condemning himself by walking away from the true gospel to a false, so-called gospel (Galatians 1:6-9; Philippians 3:2-3).

The apostle Paul wrote that anyone who brings you a different gospel is condemned. Paul called those visitors from Jerusalem "the men of the circumcision." He said they were malicious workers, like hungry animals. Because of their false gospel of circumcision of the flesh, Paul called them the mutilation party and told them, "Why stop there? Just go ahead and cut the whole thing off" (Galatians 5:12).

Paul wrote that outward physical signs like circumcision of the flesh don't make you a member of the family of faith in Jesus Christ. But rather, it's the inward circumcision of the heart, which involves your saving faith in Christ, and your becoming a new creation through Christ's indwelling Holy Spirit, which then enables you to obey God (John 3:3; Romans 2:28-29; 1 Corinthians 7:19; Galatians 6:15).

In Galatians 2:14, Paul also said that Peter "lived like" the ones saved by faith alone. Some mistakenly think "lived like" means Peter ate pork. "Live like" means "live forever like" those who are saved by faith (John 11:25; 1 John 4:9; see Luke 10:25 and 28).

 Sometimes "eat with" doesn't mean eat with. Peter "ate with" Gentiles means they had Christian fellowship, not pork.

Jesus ate with sinners. Does that mean Jesus participated in their sins? Of course not. Jesus ate with sinners in order to bring them to salvation, but Jesus never joined them in their sins (Mark 2:14-17; 1 Peter 2:22).

What's the devil really like?

Popular culture paints a false image of the devil as a scary looking creature with horns, hooves, and a pitchfork. But if the devil looked like that, would he fool anybody? No, we'd say, "Look, it's the devil."

The devil isn't a clown in a red jumpsuit. He knows how to trick you — if you let him. He'd love for you to think he's frightfully ugly and that he hangs out in dark, dirty places. That way you won't recognize him as he really is, and you won't see him in the places where he *does* hang out. All the better for him to make a fool of you.

The devil possesses super intelligence. The devil juggles words like a magician to catch you in his trap (Daniel 8:23-25; 2 Corinthians 2:11; 1 Timothy 3:7).

The devil has a suitcase full of disguises. He can trick you by appearing to be a good angel. And his greatest trick will be making people think he's Jesus Christ. The devil is called the Antichrist. "Anti" means "instead of." The devil will come instead of Christ and be worshipped as Christ, until the real Christ returns and destroys him. The Antichrist will look like Jesus Christ, and will imitate Christ (2 Corinthians 11:14; 1 John 2:18; Revelation 13:11).

The devil will perform miracles. He will trick people by making fire come down from the sky, probably while saying, "Praise God." People will say, "Look! It's Jesus!" (2 Thessalonians 2:1-12; Revelation 13:13-15).

The devil is beautiful. Ezekiel 28:11-15 calls the devil the king of Tyrus, and says he's the most beautiful person you've ever seen — and that he was in Eden. You didn't think Eve was tricked into disobeying God by a talking snake, did you? No, Eve was deceived by a supernaturally clever, dazzlingly beautiful, extraordinarily talented con man — who was none other than the devil himself.

But the Bible says in Genesis 3:1 that it was a *serpent* who talked to Eve. Yes, and in Revelation 12:9 the devil is called a *dragon*. You don't think Eve spoke with a dragon, do you? No, when the Bible refers to the devil as a serpent and a dragon, and to his co-workers as snakes and scorpions, it's vivid language to make us see how dangerous they are. Jesus referred to Herod as "that fox" (Luke 13:32), but we know that means Herod was a devious person, not actually a fox. Doesn't Genesis 3:14 say the serpent will crawl on his belly and eat dust? That sure sounds like an actual snake. Yes, it does, but by looking in other places in the Bible you'll see that it's poetic language depicting someone who has suffered utter defeat (Psalm 44:25; 72:9).

The devil is a liar and a murderer, and he's coming for you

The devil wants to get you to lose your life — eternal life. He does that by stealing the Word of God which saves a person's soul. The devil wants you to become like him and sin against God (Mark 4:15; John 8:44; Romans 10:17; 2 Corinthians 11:3; Ephesians 2:2-8; James 1:14; 1 Peter 5:8-9).

 The devil's most effective weapon is confusion, and he hides in causes that sound good but are evil.

But the devil can't make you sin. Always remember that. Jesus said, "Don't be gullible" (Matthew 24:4).

The Bible says Christians are engaged in a spiritual war with powerful evil spirits. But we don't fight the devil ourselves; rather, we resist him. We ask Jesus to rescue us from the devil, and we let Jesus do the fighting. We can be victorious over the devil through Christ. And yes, that old Serpent called the devil and Satan will suffer utter defeat when his head is crushed by Jesus (Genesis 3:15; Zechariah 3:2; Matthew 6:13; Hebrews 2:14; Jude 1:9; Revelation 20:10).

What is the mark of the Beast?

The mark of the Beast is not a chip in your right hand or a tattoo on your forehead. It's much deeper than that.

What's in it for the devil if he puts a chip in your right hand or a tattoo on your forehead? Not much.

Those who receive the mark of the Beast are those who join the devil's religion. The devil will cause there to be only one religion in the whole world, and he will be the god of that religion.

Revelation 13:11-18 says the devil will come to earth as someone called the Second Beast, who is also called the False Prophet and the Antichrist, and *he will cause (almost) everyone to receive a mark on their right hand or on their forehead*. The Bible gives the devil many names: the god of this world, the Father of Lies, the Vile Person, the Prince that shall come, the Son of Perdition, the Lawless One, the Man of Sin, etc. It's all the same personage — the devil (Daniel 9:26; 11:21; John 8:44; 2 Corinthians 4:4; 2 Thessalonians 2:3, 8; 1 John 2:18; Revelation 19:20).

Revelation 13:12 says the False Prophet will cause (almost) the whole world to worship the First Beast. Think of it like this: the False Prophet is the false Jesus, the First Beast is the devil's religion (which was preceded by the devil's worldwide government) and the Dragon is the devil as the false god. Whatever you call him, whatever role he plays, the bottom line is that the devil wants you to worship him as though he were God (Isaiah 14:14; Matthew 4:9; 2 Thessalonians 2:4; Revelation 13:4).

The devil used to be one of God's best angels. But it went to his head. He envied God and wanted to be worshipped like God. And he convinced a third of God's children to join him in a rebellion against God (Isaiah 14:12-15; Ezekiel 28:12-18; Revelation 12:3-4).

So, what is this mark of the Beast?

Sometimes the Bible uses "right hand" symbolically to refer to your actions, what you're working for, and "forehead" for what's in your mind, what you care about and love (Numbers 9:23; Deuteronomy 11:18).

The mark of the Beast on the right hand or forehead, means a person is using their mind and actions to do the devil's work.

> A chip or a tattoo can't take away your faith in Jesus. When you belong to Jesus, nothing can take you away from Him (Romans 8:35-39).

You've got to prepare now by getting to know the true Jesus so you won't think the False Prophet is Jesus and worship *him*. Those of us who belong to Jesus have to do our part. We worship God by studying and meditating on the Bible and obeying what it says. Then God will put His seal of approval on us; He puts His Holy Spirit in our hearts. Jesus writes our names in His Book of Life (eternal life), and He writes God's name on our foreheads (Ezekiel 9:4; Ephesians 1:13; Revelation 7:3; 20:4).

The devil will harass us but he won't defeat us because we have Christ on our side. We resist the devil, and we will live forever with Jesus (Matthew 24:13; Ephesians 4:27; 6:11; Philippians 4:13; James 4:7; 1 John 5:4).

The devil will be a tyrant toward those who do his work. They will be tormented by sin and will not have the peace that Jesus gives. They will all perish together, body and soul. Those who receive the mark, along with their god, the devil, will be gone, forever.
(John 14:27; Acts 10:38; 2 Timothy 2:26; Revelation 20:10,15)

Christians are to be vigilant — ready, watching, and waiting for the true Christ, our Lord and Savior, who loves us and gave His life for us (Matthew 24:42-44; 25:13; Luke 21:36; Romans 5:8; 1 John 3:16).

What does the Bible mean by "tongues"?

Senseless acts like speaking in a way that has no meaning, or falling to the floor like a clown, are *not* evidence that someone has God's Holy Spirit. The evidence that someone has the Holy Spirit is something the Bible calls the "fruit of the Spirit." "Fruit" means results, and Galatians 5:22-23 (KJV) tells us what happens to a person, over time, when God gives them His Holy Spirit: *"... the fruit of the Spirit is love, joy, peace, longsuffering, gentleness, goodness, faith, meekness, temperance."*

There are Christians who make ungodly, meaningless sounds from their mouths, a practice they call "speaking in tongues" or "personal prayer languages." They say God is causing them to produce those bizarre sounds — even though the Bible nowhere instructs believers to do such things — even though the Bible *condemns* doing such things — even though no righteous person in the Bible ever did such things — even though the only ones who do such things are fake mediums, the demon-possessed, and practitioners of voodooistic religions who allow evil spirits to enter them and speak through them.

This means then, that those so-called personal prayer languages are *not* from God; they are instead from the Evil One — they are, in fact, devil's tongues (Isaiah 8:19; Matthew 6:7; 1 Timothy 6:20-21).

The devil's-tongues speakers wrench 1 Corinthians chapter 14 out of context, and claim it says something completely opposite to what Paul *is* teaching. In that chapter, Paul is instructing the church to not allow disorder during their meetings. In verses 1-33, Paul is simply saying, if you and your friends come to church and you speak a language no one else understands, then just sit down and be quiet and don't be disturbing everybody. In verse 2, Paul says "you are speaking to God." He's making the same point in verse 9, where he says "you're speaking to the air." *It's sarcasm.* God knows all languages. But people don't, so you're talking to the air.

Suppose someone took verse 9 out of context and told people that God wants them to talk to air? Kind of ridiculous, right? But devil's-tongues speakers want you to believe that in verse 2, Paul told us to teach the deep truths of the Bible to God — like raving lunatics! (And God doesn't need you to teach Him the Bible, thank you.)

 God *does* want us to teach the deep truths of the Bible to each other — humbly, in simple words, *in languages people understand.* That's the love Paul talked about in 1 Corinthians chapter 13. That's the context.

The day of Pentecost, Acts chapter 2, was about God's love through Jesus Christ no longer belonging to just the nation of Israel, and the gospel now being shared with all people. It was to show that a believer no longer needed to go to the temple and to the Levitical priests who acted between them and God, and were only symbolic of the coming reality.

The 120 disciples, "ordinary" people — laymen, if you will — now *they* were the priests who spoke about God. And they were not speaking in Hebrew, the holy language of the temple, which the visitors to Jerusalem didn't understand. Instead the disciples spoke boldly and fearlessly about the wonderful works of God in the ordinary languages (tongues) of the people — the Greek and Aramaic dialects which they and the people were familiar with (1 Peter 2:9).

That was the miracle in Acts chapter 2 — that boldness and fearlessness in speaking was the power from on high given to the disciples when they received the indwelling Holy Spirit. It was the visible evidence that the reality, Christ, had fulfilled what the temple symbolized.

Our God doesn't use meaningless gibberish. Jesus Christ is the Word of God, the *Logos*, which means Jesus and His true followers speak clearly, logically, and intelligently, using words to appeal to the minds and hearts of those who hear them. Christians are to reject fables and build each other up with truths from the Bible (2 Timothy 3:15-4:4).

Does God work "signs and wonders" through Christians today?

Watch out for Christians who say that God is working "signs and wonders" through them. They give people false hope of being instantly healed. What they're doing is criminal. It's spiritual fraud.

When the Christian church began, God did miraculous things called signs and wonders through the hands of the apostles of Jesus. People were healed and dead people were made alive. You may have met some who claim that God does the same miracles through *them* that He did through the apostles. They are frauds.

Why do I say they're frauds? The best evidence we have that God's not doing through them what He did through the apostles is the fact that God's not doing through them what He did through the apostles.

Here's what a real sign looks like
There was a man who had been physically disabled his whole life. He had never walked or stood on his feet. All he could do was sit at the gate of the temple and beg. One day, two of the apostles, Peter and John, went to the temple. The man asked them for money. Peter said to him, "I don't have any money, but I'll give you what I do have: in the name of Jesus Christ of Nazareth, rise up and walk." Then Peter took the man by the hand, and immediately he was healed. The man walked into the temple with Peter and John, jumping for joy and praising God. All the people who saw what happened were stunned because they knew the man had been disabled from birth (Acts 3:1-12).

When Christians try to do that now, all they end up with is a person who's still physically disabled, and who now thinks Christianity is a scam.

Should we pray for each other? Of course. God might heal us, or He might not. But I'm talking about signs done by God.

 Signs done by God had meaning and purpose, and were done as God saw fit, through men who were leaders. When people were healed, it was instantly and completely.

God doesn't do it on demand or because you can say a prayer as though you're auditioning for the role of Hamlet.

When God sent Moses to the children of Israel, God told Moses to perform signs which would prove he was speaking for God. Moses picked up a dangerous snake by the tail and it turned into a shepherd's staff. It would be ridiculous for someone to say they can perform the signs that Moses performed (Exodus 4:1-9; 29-31).

Centuries later, God once again needed to use signs. Acts 2:22 tells us that God's purpose in the signs that Jesus performed was to show that Jesus is the Lord, the Messiah, the Anointed One. (Matthew 11:2-6; John 3:2; 5:36; 7:31; 10:25, 37-38)

And in Hebrews 2:3-4 we're told that God performed supernatural signs through the hands of the apostles to show the people who it was that He had chosen: they were to be the leaders of the early Church, and the men who would write a whole new section of Scripture, the New Testament, which would complete the Bible. There would be no new Scripture after the apostles died. (Acts 5:12-16; 2 Corinthians 12:12; Jude 1:3)

> Jesus restored sight to the blind.
> God used the apostles Peter and Paul to bring people back from death (Matthew 10:1; 15:30-31; Acts 9:36-42; 20:9-12).
> It's ridiculous for someone to say they can perform the signs and wonders that Jesus and the apostles performed.

Is the Sabbath a day of the week ?

A man in Harvard Square told me Saturday is the seventh day of the week and that I should respect it more than the other six days. Why? He said it's because that was the day when Jesus taught in the temple. Certain sects teach that. It's an absurd and offensive false teaching. So I responded to the man's admonition by telling him about a bank robber who was asked, "Why do you rob banks?" and who replied, "Because that's where the money is."

Why did Jesus teach in the temple on the seventh day? Because that's where His people, the lost sheep of Israel, were. They met in the temple on the seventh day to learn about God, so that's when Jesus went there to teach them. That poor man I met in Harvard Square has been deceived by a Christian sect that misdirects their people away from Jesus and to a day of the week. Jesus also taught while sitting in a boat. I hope no one has started a Christian sect based on sitting in boats.

What is the Sabbath?

If you're asking, "What *is* the Sabbath?" then the answer is, "Jesus Christ is the Sabbath." The word "sabbath" means rest. *Christians rest in Jesus, not just on Saturday, but every day.* To rest in Christ means we put our trust in Him for our salvation (Hebrews 4:10).

What *was* the Sabbath?

The answer to the question, "What *was* the Sabbath?" is, "A day of the week was the Sabbath." In the Old Testament, God told the children of Israel that they were to only work six days a week. The seventh day was to be set apart as a day of rest (Exodus 16:21-26).

Didn't God say to observe the seventh day *forever*?

Yes, in Exodus 31:12-16, God told the children of Israel that they were to take very seriously His law instructing them to only work six days and then rest on the seventh day. And God said they must continue to obey that law — *forever*.

God also told Israel to kill a lamb *forever*

When God was about to kill all the firstborn in Egypt, He told the children of Israel there was something they could do that would cause Him to spare their firstborn. God said each family must kill a lamb and put its blood on the door of their house. They obeyed God's instruction and all of Israel's firstborn were spared. God told Israel they were to remember what He did for them in Egypt by killing a lamb every year on that date. The lamb they killed was called the Passover lamb. Israel remembered the first Passover when death passed over all the houses that had the blood of the lamb on the door. And God said they were to kill a lamb every year — forever (Exodus 12:14).

Yes, *forever*

The way the nation of Israel worshipped God was only a temporary pattern of what was to come. The Passover and the Sabbath are observed forever in Jesus Christ — by the *true* Israel, which is *anyone* who believes in the Lord Jesus (Hebrews 7:11-19; 8:1-13; 9:11; 10:1).

The symbol and the reality

The Passover lamb that Israel killed and the day of the week they observed were only *symbols* of what was to come in the *reality* — Jesus Christ. Christians don't kill a lamb every year because Jesus Christ is our Passover Lamb. Jesus gave Himself as a sacrifice one time to pay for sin (1 Corinthians 5:7; 1 Peter 3:18).

 And Christians don't rest on one day of the week like Israel did, because *Jesus Christ is our rest* (compare Hebrews 3:11, 18-19 with Hebrews 4:9-11).

I wonder if the man in Harvard Square kills a lamb every year?

You're going backwards if you observe the seventh day like Israel did. It's just as absurd and offensive as it would be if you killed a Passover lamb. It's saying Jesus isn't enough. You're taking your focus off Christ and putting it on a day of the week. The apostle Paul used the Greek word *stoicheia* to compare your practice to pagans who worship spirits in trees and mountains (Galatians 4:8-10).

Were the early Christians practicing socialism?

Young people in America are being indoctrinated by certain professors and politicians to believe that capitalism is evil and socialism will produce an ideal society. Americans have enjoyed freedom for so long we don't appreciate what we have.

When the Christian church was just getting started, all the Christians were living in Jerusalem. We learn from the Book of Acts that the Christian believers did not consider any of their possessions to be their own property, but rather they all held everything in common. There weren't any needy people among them because those who owned land or houses were selling them and bringing the money to the apostles. Then the money was distributed to each according to their need (Acts 2:32-35; 44-45).

Sounds exactly like socialism, doesn't it?
But it's not socialism. A socialist government *forcibly* takes the fruit of people's labor — their property and goods — and redistributes it to others. The early Christians gave out of love and compassion for their fellow Christians. It was 100% voluntary. It's Christian love.

> They behaved as though the whole group
> was one body with one heart and soul   - Acts 4:32

The apostle Peter told Ananias that the land he owned was his own property, and if he sold it the money was his to use however he wished (Acts 5:4). That's not socialism.

In 2 Corinthians 8:3, the apostle Paul used the Greek word *authairetos* to praise how Christians gave to other Christians. It's #830 in the Greek dictionary in the back of the *Strong's Concordance*. It's made up of two words: # 846, *autos*, which means "self." And #138, *haireomai*, which means to make your own choice.

So Paul was saying that *giving was a voluntary, personal decision*. It was something they were under no obligation to do. That's the opposite of socialism.

There's no commandment to share everything in common

It's wrong to think we have to live the way the early Christians did. When the church first began they had just received the indwelling Holy Spirit and the apostles were still alive. That was then, this is now. Also, those first Christians met together in their own private homes (Acts 2:46). Of course people kept their homes. Lydia was a businesswoman who owned her own home (Acts 16:14-15, 40). The houses and lands the early Christians sold to help the needy were extra properties they weren't using.

The God-given right to life, liberty, and the pursuit of happiness

The values highly esteemed in the Bible are those consistent with a capitalist system of government and *opposed* to the practices of a socialist government. Proverbs 31:10-31 praises a virtuous wife who owns a field where she planted a vineyard. She is a successful businesswoman, a capitalist (see Psalms 128:1-4). She would have lost her enthusiasm under a socialist government that took away the fruits of her labor. Proverbs 16:26 explains that people will work because of a hunger inside them. They work for their own incentive, for their own rewards.

It's a beautiful thing, very pleasing, to see people eat and drink and enjoy all the good things they've acquired because of the hard work they do during their time on this earth. Those good things are given to them by God to be their own property, their possessions.

> *It is the gift of God to every person to whom God has given wealth and treasures. And with those treasures God has given them the right that they alone have the power and authority to control those possessions of theirs.*
>
> *It is in that way that they can enjoy great happiness from the fruit of their labor.*
>
> - Ecclesiastes 5:18-19

Proverbs 13:22 says it's *good* for a person to grow wealthy enough so that they can leave an inheritance not only to their children but also their grandchildren. That's the beauty of freedom.

Did Jesus promote socialism?

No, Jesus did not promote socialism. One of His disciples was Joseph of Arimathaea, a wealthy man. Jesus never told him it was wrong to be wealthy. Jesus never told him to redistribute his wealth or give it to the state to redistribute. In the Old Testament there's a prophecy that Jesus would be buried with the rich. Joseph of Arimathaea — a rich man — gave his own tomb for Jesus to be buried. The prophesy could not have been fulfilled without a rich man among the disciples of Jesus. Joseph and Nicodemus anointed the body of Jesus with a vast quantity of expensive ointments that only the rich could afford, and buried Him in Joseph's tomb (Isaiah 53:9; Matthew 27:57-60; John 19:39-40).

Jesus wasn't a socialist

Jesus didn't come to redistribute wealth. Jesus came to save people from their sins (Matthew 1:21).

What is separation of church and state?

The First Amendment does *not* give government the power to silence religious expression. On the contrary, it was written to guarantee citizens the right to free expression of religion and to make freedom of conscience the law of the land.

Little children in a public school in America were planning to sing a song during their Thanksgiving performance. The song contained a few words thanking God for His blessings. But a pro-atheism group sent a letter to the school's superintendent to complain about the song. They claimed that singing such a song in a public school would violate the First Amendment to the Constitution, and go against "the separation of church and state." The superintendent wrote back and told them they were right, and that he would be more diligent in the future to uphold the law. He then told the children they could not celebrate Thanksgiving by singing a song which thanked God for His blessings.

America's founders would be angered and disgusted at how that ignorant school superintendent let himself be conned.

What is the First Amendment?
When America became a nation our founders wrote a document called the Constitution. It provided the foundation for the laws and principles by which America would be governed. They later added Ten Amendments to the Constitution which are called the Bill of Rights. The First Amendment protects the right to freedom of religion. There's nothing mentioned about separation of church and state in the First Amendment, which simply says:

Congress shall make no law respecting an establishment of religion, (the Establishment Clause) **or prohibit the free exercise thereof.** (the Free Exercise Clause)

That school superintendent was swayed by a false interpretation of the First Amendment. Here's how the founders worded an earlier draft:

> *"The civil rights of none shall be abridged on account of religious belief or worship, nor shall any national religion be established, nor shall the full and equal rights of conscience be in any manner, or on any pretext, infringed."*

Why was this so important to America's founders?
America's founders wanted to prevent what happened in England, where an official state religion was enforced, the Church of England. America was to be a place of religious liberty where no one would be forced by the state to belong to a certain denomination, and no one could be prevented by the state from exercising their religious beliefs. The religion clauses in the First Amendment were not made so the government could restrict the rights of the people. Instead, they were meant to leave the citizen free to choose any religion they wanted, and to express it in any way they chose, without state interference.

Where did "separation of church and state" come from?
Thomas Jefferson, the principal author of America's Declaration of Independence, received a letter from the Danbury Baptist Association in 1801, while he was serving as president. They wanted Jefferson's assurance that America's founding documents would guarantee them the freedom to worship according to their denomination. Jefferson responded that there was a "wall of separation between Church and State." He used a metaphor taken from a well-known sermon, "The Garden and the Wilderness," delivered by Baptist preacher Roger Williams, founder of the state of Rhode Island.

 The wall of separation was meant to protect "the Garden of the Church" from being overrun by "the Wilderness of Government." *Thomas Jefferson used that expression to assure the Danbury Baptists that the government could NOT interfere in their worship.*

Did the founders worship God in the public arena?
Yes, overwhelmingly so.

In 1789, President **George Washington**, the father of our country, read a Thanksgiving Day proclamation in which he asked God to bless America.

Two of the most important founders attended weekly Christian church services in the Capitol, the meeting place of America's Congress. They were **Thomas Jefferson**, the main author of America's Declaration of Independence, and **James Madison**, the principal author of America's Constitution.

A man named **Fisher Ames** is considered to be the author of the Establishment Clause. He publicly said the Bible should be the leading text in America's schools. And in 1777, **Congress** approved the purchase of 20,000 Bibles to distribute to the states.

Our founders welcomed God into our government because they knew that God had His hand in the formation of America. They knew that for America to survive and flourish they would need God in the midst of our government and schools. That's not the same as establishing a law to make a state religion. It's having leaders who know and respect the one true God of the Bible, and who enact laws in accordance with His standards.

For nearly 150 years after Jefferson wrote his famous letter, the courts maintained the position that the wall of separation between church and state was to *protect* public religious expressions, not to limit them.

What happened to reverse this protection?
A Supreme Court ruling in 1947 in *Everson v. Board of Education* imposed a radical change on the meaning of separation of church and state. The Supreme Court cited only Jefferson's "wall of separation between Church and State" metaphor, ignored the rest of his letter and it's clear context, and turned the historic use of that phrase on its head.

The judges of the Supreme Court announced a new policy: this separation phrase would now NOT be used to *protect* public religious expressions, but instead it would be used as a reason to *exclude* them, and eliminate a person's right to religious expression in all public places.

This made the First Amendment a limitation on individuals rather than a limitation on government.

What is happening now?

There are people who want to remove the Bible, silence Christians, and eradicate Christianity because it is the source of all the good in the world. What they're really doing is replacing one ideology with another, one set of beliefs with another. They want atheism to replace Christianity. They're forcing Americans to let atheism into our government and schools, and banish Christianity — to drive out and eradicate Christian principles of right and wrong, and replace them with their "religion" of atheism.

By basing our laws on the morality of the Bible, our founders created the best possible nation. We've seen a steady decline in society since prayer and Bibles were removed from school. Evil forces are taking away our freedoms gradually. America is suffering because of it. America could repent. But the Bible says the contrary will happen; things will only get worse. Americans will be put into bondage by a people who will rise up from among them (Deuteronomy 28:43; Psalm 33:12; Amos 8:11; 2 Timothy 3:1-5).

If we bring the Bible back into our government and schools then our military and economy will be strengthened. We could fight America's opioid crisis armed with the spiritual tools our society needs.

The First Amendment was written to protect the rights of school-children to thank God, read their Bibles, and pray — in school or any other place they choose. Citing it as a reason to prevent them from doing so would be seen by our founders as a perversion of its intent and an act done by criminals.

Chapter Twelve

Beyond the Brazil Nut Factor

Don't lean on your own understanding,
but trust in God with all your thoughts and plans,
all your heart.

Wherever you go, seek God's wisdom,
and He will lead you to the right path.

- Proverbs 3:5-6

Bible Quiz questions

The following are some of the questions I came up with for the Bible Quiz street ministry.

As I'd tell people at the Quiz, I'm not trying to see how much you know or put you on the spot. I don't expect you to know the answers to all the questions. I ask them because I'm hoping that when I tell you the answer you'll learn something or be surprised.

Quizzing a Brown University student at the corner of Thayer and Angell, Providence, RI

Multiple choice

100. Who parted the Red Sea?

    A. Aaron

    B. Moses

    C. Joshua

    D. None of the above

101. What must you do to be saved?

    A. Believe in the Lord Jesus Christ

    B. Get baptized with water

    C. Join a local church

    D. Do everything the leaders of your church tell you to do

    E. All of the above

102. Who said these words:

"It is more blessed to give than to receive."

    A. Benjamin Franklin

    B. Huck Finn

    C. Franklin Roosevelt

    D. Jesus

[Answers on next page]

100. D. None of the above
The following verses tell us who parted the Red Sea. **It was God**: Exodus
14:21; 15:8; Joshua 4:23; Nehemiah 9:9-11; Psalm 66:6; 74:13; 78:13; 106:9; 136:13;
Isaiah 63:12. God parts the waters, heals the sick, and raises the dead. Did
you think Moses parted the Red Sea? We always have to go to the Bible to
confirm everything.

**101. A. The only way you can be saved is by believing in the Lord Jesus
Christ**. Salvation can't be given to you by a church or denomination. Water
baptism won't save you (Acts 16:30-31; Romans 10:9-11; Ephesians 2:8-9).

102. D. Jesus
Although it's not recorded in the four Gospels that Jesus said these words,
the apostle Paul told us that Jesus said them. Paul wrote to the elders of
the church at Ephesus, "Let us remember these words of the Lord Jesus,
'It is more blessed to give than to receive'" (Acts 20:35).

Jesus and the apostles

103. In Matthew 24:4, Jesus gave us a warning. He said, "Beware, never let anyone do (this) to you." Do what?

104. What was the first message given by Jesus when He started His ministry? It was also the first message given by John the Baptist, the apostle Peter, and the disciples of Jesus when they started their ministries. In one word — what did they tell people to do?

105. In Acts chapter 5, the apostles were arrested for teaching people about Jesus. They were given a severe beating and released. As they walked away, they rejoiced. Why did they rejoice?

106. What did Jesus say is the most important of God's command-ments? Hint: It's not one of the Ten Commandments, but Jesus *was* quoting the Old Testament: Deuteronomy 6:5, 10:12, and 30:6.

107. The Greek word *thaumazo* means to be amazed or to marvel at something. The Bible only uses *thaumazo* twice to describe amazement felt by Jesus: once when He heard the positive words of a certain man, and another time when He heard the negative words of a group of people. What were the two opposite qualities that Jesus marvelled at?

108. What is the only miracle besides the resurrection of Jesus that is recorded in all four Gospels?

109. What was Jesus' father's name?

[Answers on next page]

103. Jesus warned **"do not let anyone deceive you,"** (lead you astray).

104. They said, **"Repent."** The word "repent" literally means to change your mind. So when they told people to repent, it meant to change their mind about their sin and turn to Jesus to be forgiven and cleansed (Matthew 3:1-2; 4:17; Mark 6:12; Acts 2:38).

105. They rejoiced **because God considered them worthy to suffer for Christ** (Acts 5:41 and 1 Peter 4:13).

106. Jesus said the most important of God's commandments is: **"You must love the Lord your God with all your heart, and with all your soul, and with all your mind, and with all your strength"** (Mark 12:30).

107. Jesus marvelled at the **great faith** of a Roman centurion (Matthew 8:8-10) and at the **great unbelief** of the people in His home town (Mark 6:6).

108. The only miracle besides the resurrection of Christ from the dead that is recorded in all four Gospels is **the feeding of 5,000 men** and their families from five loaves and two fishes (Matthew 14:19-21; Mark 6:41-44; Luke 9:14-17; John 6:9-13). It is a Hebrew idiom to repeat something for emphasis. The fact that this miracle is reported four times suggests that it is important. Just as Jesus gave the loaves and fishes to the apostles who then distributed them to the people, Jesus also gave the Word of God to the apostles to distribute.

109. Did you say Joseph was Jesus' father's name? My answer is: **God.** Jesus wasn't conceived by Joseph. Jesus was conceived by the Holy Spirit. And every time Jesus prayed to God, Jesus called God "Father." Joseph was the father of Jesus only as a matter of law; Joseph was the legal guardian of Jesus when Jesus was a child. And because of that Jesus was obedient to Joseph (Luke 2:48-52; John 17:1).

Can you name them?

110. Can you name the two in the Bible who said,
"I am the first and the last."?

111. Who bit the apple first, Adam or Eve?

112. Tell me who said these words:
"Fear the LORD and serve Him sincerely and faithfully ...
And if the thought of serving the LORD displeases you,
then choose today who it is you will serve ...
But as for me and my house, we will serve the LORD."

113. On two different occasions in the New Testament, a man
asked God to forgive those who were executing him on false
charges. Can you name the two men?

114. In Exodus 9:16, God said the following about someone:
"The reason I appointed you was to show My power, and
so that I would become known throughout all the earth."
Who did God say that about?

115. Who is the "queen of heaven"?

116. What are the names of the four women from the Old
Testament who were included in the genealogy of Jesus
(Matthew 1:3-6)?

117. Who carried the cross to the place where Jesus was crucified?

[Answers on next page]

110. In Isaiah 44:6, **God the Father** said, "I am the first, and I am the last," and in Revelation 1:17, **Jesus** said, "I am the first and the last." They're the only ones who said it, and the only ones who *could* say it. What can we conclude from that? Jesus is God.

111. Adam and Eve didn't bite an apple (Genesis 3:6). Apples aren't mentioned in the Bible until Proverbs 25:11. My point? Don't believe everything you hear without checking it out for yourself.

112. **Joshua** said those words to the children of Israel after they had taken the land of Canaan (Joshua 24:14-15).

113. **Jesus**, during His crucifixion, and **Stephen**, as he was being stoned to death, both asked God to forgive their killers (Luke 23:34; Acts 7:60).

114. God said that about **Pharaoh of Egypt** (Exodus 9:16).

115. The so-called "queen of heaven" appears in the Bible in Jeremiah 7:18 and 44:17-19. It's the name for **a pagan goddess** which the children of Israel started worshipping in defiance of God. Mary, the mother of Jesus, is not the queen of heaven.

116. The genealogy of Jesus in Matthew chapter 1 includes **Tamar** (verse 3), **Rahab** (verse 5), **Ruth** (verse 5) and **Bathsheba** (verse 6) where she is called "her that had been the wife of Uriah."

117. The Gospels of Matthew, Mark, and Luke say the cross Jesus would be crucified on was carried by **Simon of Cyrene**. The Gospel of John says the cross was carried by **Jesus**. Some look at that and accuse the Bible of having contradictions. But it's not a contradiction. The answer is simple — they both carried it (Matthew 27:32; Mark 15:21; Luke 23:26; John 19:16-17).

Can you name them?

118. There is only one who is to be called "Holy Father" and no one else. Who is the Holy Father?

119. Can you name four individuals the Bible says were influenced by the devil to do wrong?

120. Name two in the Bible who God let die before national calamity came, because they were good.

121. Tell me three in the Bible who were called "a man of war."

122. Second Peter 2:7-9 says that a certain man's righteous soul was "vexed daily" from seeing and hearing the filthy things that the lawless people of his city were doing. Who was the man?

123. In Numbers 21:5-6, the children of Israel told Moses they hated the manna that God was feeding them. They said it was disgusting. Because of that, God sent fiery serpents to bite them and many died. Hating the manna was a serious offense because of who the manna represented. Who did the manna represent?

124. What was the source of Samson's strength?

Why 40 years?

125. Why did God choose forty as the number of years Israel would wander in the wilderness?

[Answers on next page]

118. In John 17:11, Jesus called God "Holy Father." **God** is our Holy Father. A man must never be called Holy Father (see Matthew 23:9).

119. The four people the devil influenced to do wrong are: **Eve** (Genesis 3:1-6); **David** (1 Chronicles 21:1-2); **Judas** (Luke 22:3-4); and **Ananias** (Acts 5:3).

120. Abijah, the son of Jeroboam (1 Kings 14:12-13), and **Josiah, king of Judah** (2 Kings 22:18-20; 2 Chronicles 34:26-28). "A righteous person dies ... and is taken away from the trouble which is to come" - Isaiah 57:1.

121. Goliath was called a man of war (1 Samuel 17:33); **David** was called a man of war (1 Samuel 16:18; 1 Chronicles 28:3); and **God** was called a man of war (Exodus 15:3).

122. Second Peter 2:7-9 says God delivered **Lot** out of the city of Sodom before God destroyed it, because Lot was righteous.

123. It was such a serious offense to call the manna disgusting because **the manna symbolized Christ**. In 1 Corinthians 10:9, the apostle Paul wrote that we must not put Christ to the test as some did, and were destroyed by serpents because of it. The manna was bread from heaven. In John chapter 6, Jesus said, "I am the Bread of Life which comes down from heaven, that anyone may eat and not die" (see John 6:31-35).

124. Did you say that Samson's hair was the source of his strength? Can hair give a person strength? No. But God can, and **God was the source** of Samson's strength (Judges 13:5; 14:5-6,19; 15:14-15). In Judges 16:22, Samson's hair began to grow back but he still called out to God for strength in verse 28 (see also Numbers 6:1-8).

125. God told the children of Israel to go into the "Promised Land" of Canaan. But they refused to go after they heard the bad report from ten of the twelve spies they'd sent to search out the land for forty days. In Numbers 14:34, God said that because of Israel's disobedience and unbelief, they would wander in the wilderness for **forty years, one year for every day they searched the land** (Exodus 3:17; Numbers 13:1-33; 14:1-4).

Fill in the blank

126. Here's a fill-in-the-blank question. Amos 8:11 "Behold, the days will come, says the Lord God, that I will send a famine in the land; not a famine of food or a famine of water, but a famine of ...."

127. Fill in the blank: 2 Timothy 3:12 "Anyone who desires to live a godly life as a disciple of Christ will be ...."

128. Fill in the blank: James 1:5 "If anyone lacks ...., then ask God, the one who gives generously to all who ask. He won't fault you for it, and it will be given to you."

129. Fill in the blank: Luke 11:27-28 says that while Jesus was teaching, a woman in the crowd called out, "Blessed is the womb that carried You, and the breasts which You nursed." Jesus replied, "On the contrary, blessed are they that ...."

130. According to Revelation 4:11, why did God create everything?

....

131. According to Isaiah 26:3, what must a person do so that God will keep them in perfect peace?

....

132. In Jeremiah 9:23-24, God said people should not rejoice because they have the wisdom, strength, or riches of this world. Who did God say *should* rejoice?

....

[Answers on next page]

126. God will send a famine of <u>hearing the words of the Lord.</u>

127. "Anyone who desires to live a godly life as a disciple of Christ will be <u>persecuted.</u>"

128. "If anyone lacks <u>wisdom,</u> then ask God, the one who gives generously to all who ask. He won't fault you for it, and it will be given to you."

129. Jesus replied, "On the contrary, blessed are they that <u>hear the word of God and keep it.</u>"

130. Revelation 4:11 says God created everything <u>because it pleased Him to do so.</u>

131. God will keep in perfect peace everyone who <u>sets their mind on Him, because they trust in Him.</u> The original language says "peace peace" - twice, for emphasis.

132. God said the one who should rejoice is <u>the one who knows and understands Him,</u> that He is the Lord, who shows lovingkindness, and who carries out justice and righteousness to everyone. That knowledge is what God wants you to have, and that's what He wants to be the joy of your heart.

Fill in the blank

133. Ecclesiastes 12:7 says that when someone dies, their body returns to the earth where it came from, and their spirit returns to ....

134. Ephesians 2:8 says we are saved by the grace of God, and we receive salvation by our faith, by believing in Jesus. And Romans 10:17 says faith comes by hearing ....
....

Yes or no?

135. Is there a woman called Lilith in the Bible?

136. Was Mary Magdalene a prostitute?

137. Does the Bible call money "the root of all evil"?

138. Did Samson commit suicide?

139. In John 2:13-17, Jesus made a whip and chased the money-changers and vendors out of the temple. Was He teaching us that it's okay to engage in civil disobedience?

[Answers on next page]

133. Ecclesiastes 12:7 says that when we die, our spirit returns to <u>God who gave it.</u>

134. Faith comes by hearing <u>the word of God</u> (Romans 10:17).

135. There is no woman called Lilith in the Bible.
The Hebrew word *lilith* does appear in Isaiah 34:14, but it means "owl." Lilith is a fictional character, the mythological first wife of Adam.

136. No, Mary Magdalene was a not a prostitute.
Luke 8:2 describes her as a woman "from whom Jesus cast out seven demons." Nowhere in the Bible is she called a prostitute.

137. No, the Bible does not say that money is the root of all evil.
The Bible says that the *love* of money is the root of all evil (1 Timothy 6:10). "Love of money" means never being satisfied and always greedy for more.

138. No, Samson did not commit suicide.
In Judges 16:28-30, Samson asked God for strength and God gave him strength. What did Samson do with that God-given strength? He used it to push down two pillars, one with each hand. That caused the building to come crashing down, killing Samson along with many of Israel's enemies. Samson gave his life for his people. In this way Samson was like Jesus who, hundreds of years later, gave His life on the cross for His people.

139. When Jesus made a whip and cleared the temple, **He was *not* engaging in civil disobedience. He was acting as God, not as a man.** That temple was His Father's house, Jesus is the Son of God, and therefore Jesus is God Himself. He had the right to clear the thieves out of God's house of prayer. Some people mistakenly teach that what Jesus did in the temple gives us the right to engage in civil disobedience such as rioting and looting. They're wrong, and if they don't repent they will answer to God for misleading people and encouraging them to commit crimes.

What does it mean?

140. According to 1 John 3:4, what is the definition of sin?

141. In Matthew 1:21, Joseph was told by the angel of the Lord to give Mary's Son the name Jesus because He will save His people from their sins. What does "Jesus" mean?

142. The birth of Jesus was prophesied in Isaiah 7:14, where it says, "A virgin will conceive and bear a Son, and will call His name Emmanuel." Over six hundred years later, Matthew 1:23 tells us the prophesy was fulfilled and gives the meaning of the name Emmanuel. What does "Emmanuel" mean?

143. What do rainbows represent?

How good do you have to be?

144. How good do you have to be to go to heaven?

[Answers on next page]

140. We sin when we **disobey the laws God has given us in the Bible.**

141. The name Jesus means **"God our Savior."**
See page 140 for the explanation of Jesus' name in Hebrew, *Yahshua*.
Matthew 1:21 says that the angel of the Lord told Joseph in a dream that his wife Mary was to call her Son's name Jesus because He will save His people from their sins. What does it mean by "His people?" His people are all those who believe in Him.

142. Matthew 1:23 says that Emmanuel means **"God with us."**

143. After the flood, when Noah's ark landed, God promised He wouldn't flood the earth again. **God said He would put the rainbow in the sky as a reminder of His promise** (Genesis 9:8-17).

144. You have to be *perfectly* **good to go to heaven**. No one is perfectly good; we all sin. But we can be judged as perfectly good and go to heaven if we're clothed with Christ's righteousness. When we receive Christ, God considers our sins to be washed away by the blood Christ shed on the cross (Isaiah 61:10; Romans 4:5; Philippians 3:9; 1 John 1:7).

Harder questions

145. Name four occasions in the Old Testament when God parted a body of water so that one or more people could walk through a sea or river on dry ground?

146. Can you tell me the two half-brothers and two second cousins who were named by God before they were born?

147. Can you tell me four different ways the Bible speaks of two witnesses?

148. In Luke 24:44-46, after Jesus rose from the dead He appeared to the eleven remaining apostles. Jesus opened their minds so they could understand the Scriptures which said that Christ would suffer, and die, and rise from the dead after three days. Jesus referred to the three parts of the Old Testament (Hebrew Bible). What are they?

149. In Matthew 4:2-4, after Jesus fasted for forty days and forty nights He was hungry.
The devil said to Him, "If you're the Son of God, then command these stones to turn into loaves of bread."
Jesus responded, "It is written, people don't live just by eating food, but by every word that comes from the mouth of God."

When Jesus said "it is written" He was referring to Deuteronomy 8:3, where God the Father said those words to the children of Israel. What was God talking about there?

[Answers on next page]

145. God parted the waters when:

(A) **Moses** led the children of Israel through the Red Sea (Exodus 14:21).

(B) **Joshua** led the children of Israel through the Jordan river (Joshua 4:23).

(C) **Elijah and Elisha** went through the Jordan river (2 Kings 2:8).

(D) **Elisha** went through the Jordan river by himself, after Elijah went to heaven in a whirlwind (2 Kings 2:14).

146. God told the parents of both **Isaac and Ishmael** the names of their children before their birth (Genesis 16:11; 17:19). Abraham was the father of both boys, but Hagar was the mother of Ishmael and Sarah was the mother of Isaac (Genesis 16:3-4; 21:1-3), so they were half-brothers. God told the parents of both **Jesus and John the Baptist** what to name their sons before they were born (Luke 1:13, 30-31). Mary, the mother of Jesus, and Elizabeth, the mother of John, were cousins (Luke 1:36). That means Jesus and John were second cousins.

147.

(A) **Two witnesses are required when certain accusations are made:** in a death penalty case (Numbers 35:30; Deuteronomy 17:6); to confront a Christian who has done wrong to a fellow Christian (Matthew 18:16); and when an accusation is made against an elder (1 Timothy 5:19).

(B) **God the Father and Jesus witness that the judgment of Jesus is true** (John 8:17-18).

(C) **The righteousness of God which is by faith in Jesus Christ is witnessed by the Law and the Prophets** (Romans 3:21-22).

(D) **God's two witnesses** (Revelation 11:3-12).

148. Jesus referred to the three divisions of the Hebrew Bible as **the Law of Moses, the Prophets, and the Psalms** (also called the Writings).

149. In Deuteronomy 8:3, God told the children of Israel **the reason why He fed them with manna** during their forty years of wandering in the wilderness. He said He did it to humble them. And that He let them be hungry, so they would learn that people don't live just by eating food, but people live by every word that comes from the mouth of the Lord.

How many?

150. When Jesus carried His cross to the place where He was crucified, how many times did He fall?

151. After Jesus resurrected from the dead, how many days did He stay on earth before He ascended into heaven?

152. Almost the last question. How many instances of resurrection in the Bible can you think of? Including individuals and groups, resurrections from the past, and ones that will happen in the future. Hint: I found twelve.

153. One night, the apostles went fishing. It was during the time when Jesus was on earth after He rose from the dead and before He went back to heaven. The apostles fished all night but caught nothing. In the morning they saw a man standing on the shore. He asked them if they had anything to eat and they said no. The man told them to cast their net off the right side of the boat. They did, and caught many fish. Then they recognized the man: it was Jesus (John 21:1-14). How many fish did they catch in their net?

[Answers on next page]

150. The Bible doesn't say that Jesus fell. Were you sure He did? That's why we must never believe anything we hear in popular culture or from the pulpit without going to the Bible to see if it's true.

151. Jesus stayed on earth for **forty days** after He resurrected from the dead, during which time He appeared to over five hundred people. And then He went back to heaven (Acts 1:1-3, 9; 1 Corinthians 15:6).

152. Resurrections in the Bible:
1] **The son of the widow of Zarephath**, with the prophet Elijah, 1 Kings 17:17-24.
2] **The son of the Shunammite woman**, with the prophet Elisha, 2 Kings 4:17-37.
3] **A dead man whose body touched the bones of Elisha** in Elisha's tomb, 2 Kings 13:20-21.
4] Jesus resurrected **the daughter of Jairus**, Mark 5:41-42.
5] Jesus resurrected **the son of the widow of Nain**, Luke 7:12-15.
6] Jesus resurrected **Lazarus**, John 11:41-44.
7] When Jesus died on the cross, graves opened and the bodies of **many saints** who had died were raised to life. They appeared to many people after Jesus was resurrected, Matthew 27:52-53.
8] **Jesus** rose from the dead, Matthew 28:6; Mark 16:6; Luke 24:6; John 20:1-31.
9] **Tabitha (also called Dorcas)**, with the apostle Peter, Acts 9:36-41.
10] **Eutychus**, with the apostle Paul, Acts 20:9-12.
11] **The first resurrection of the saints**, Luke 14:14; Revelation 20:4-6.
12] **God's two witnesses**, Revelation 11:9-11.

153. The apostles caught **153 fish** in their net (John 21:11). And that's why there's 153 questions in this book.

The search for Christian fellowship

In Chapter One, I told you that I was a baby Christian who met a street preacher named Tilman Gandy, my Brazil Nut Factor. Now, here's how I went on to have my own street ministry.

Tilman told me to read the Bible — to start at Genesis and read one chapter every day. That was smart. He knew what I could handle — he didn't overload me. And I did read one chapter a day. I made it to the Book of 1 Samuel and stopped. (It would be fifteen years before I'd start again.)

Baptism

Three years after I met Tilman, in the summer of 1986 when I turned thirty-three, he brought up baptism. I knew it was what I wanted to do. Tilman took me to a church and he and the pastor baptized me. I was fully immersed in a tank of water.

Four years later, off I went. I left Rhode Island. But by that time something was different. I realized, for the first time, that I had the Holy Spirit. God's Holy Spirit was living in my heart.

One reason I knew this is because I realized that certain things I was doing were actually sinful. The Holy Spirit was telling me they were sinful. I wanted to stop doing them but I couldn't, and I didn't know why. I would find out later though, why I couldn't stop.

Back to the Bible

Something happened in the summer of 1998, the year I turned forty-five. God touched my heart again. I suddenly felt strong feelings of regret that I'd stopped reading the Bible. God gave me a strong desire to start reading the Bible again. For two years I read every day, and for the first time I read the whole Bible all the way through.

After two years of reading the Bible I realized something — it isn't enough to just *read* the Bible. You also have to study the Bible. But how?

I've always done things in a simple way. So when I decided I needed to study the Bible, I went out and bought books like commentaries and lexicons, and I listened to Bible teachers on TV. God directed my steps, and I put together a nice little library of books to help me in my study of the Bible.

When I started studying, the biggest thing yet happened. Now I knew what had been missing. I learned why I couldn't get free of certain habitual sins. It was because before, I didn't have the Bible, the Word of God. But now I had the Spirit *and* the Word.

I experienced a dramatic change. I was much less of a miserable wretch than I'd been before. Some of those sins I'd committed habitually for decades just disappeared. I hated those sins. Now I felt God's power and blessings. Now I could walk in the Spirit. I had a way to get the ability to avoid sin. You've got to have both, the Spirit *and* the Word.

The power in the Bible
It's beautiful the way God arranged this. He is the source of grace, salvation, power, and holiness. He does it. But if we don't act then it's not going to happen. We have to do our part. I was at war now with my sin, and I had victories and losses. Christians fight the war between the Spirit and the flesh every day, our whole lives, with God's help.

My mind was so happy to be receiving and meditating on the Bible. I was a dry sponge soaking up the Living Water of God's Word. God was gradually giving me knowledge, understanding, and wisdom, and He was changing me, cleaning me up, and renewing my mind through His Word. Bible study is medicine for what ails you. When you receive Christ, and God gives you His Holy Spirit, then you can go to the Bible anytime for comfort, peace, joy, cleansing, discernment, and direction. And God has given us Bible study as a weapon against the temptation to sin. As we go on we develop an intense hatred of sin, and an intense desire for holiness.

Looking for Christian fellowship

For the first time in my life, in my late forties, I had something to use my mind for, something I loved. I studied the Bible for hours each day. I did this from 2000 to 2007. Then I wanted so much to find others who'd had the same experience I'd had. I wanted to talk to them, compare notes, learn from them — I craved Christian fellowship.

My experience in churches

Naively, I thought churches were the place to go to find people who love God's Word. So I went to church services and Bible studies. But I was stunned and sickened by what I found. It was like they didn't know about the experience I'd had. It was like they saw the Bible as just one of the things a church does. The Bible had been removed from its proper place of reverence.

The pastors weren't impressing upon their people the utter, indispensable importance of the Bible. They weren't teaching them that they *have* to study, and they weren't teaching them *how* to study. The pastors made the people feel like they were unworthy.

In the dozen or more churches I went to, I met so many people who had been made to think they weren't worthy — that only those who have a degree from a Bible school and have been approved by the church can study, come to conclusions, interpret, and teach the Bible.

"Fellowship time"

At one of the churches I went to, the schedule said there was a time called "Fellowship." I was so naive, I thought they would be sitting around a table with their Bibles open, discussing the sermon. Instead, they were standing around having the same kind of conversations you could find in a barber shop. And when I'd try to talk about something in the Bible they'd act shocked, disgusted. It was that "unworthy" thing, and a bizarre loyalty to the pastor, as though talking theology would be some sort of unfaithfulness to the pastor.

Being with fellow Christians and not talking about things from the Bible was unbearable for me. I attended that church for a month, it was all I could take. After a month I felt spiritually sick, anemic. I wanted to just go back to studying on my own, get back into God's Word to regain my spiritual health. The people in churches are given just enough Bible to make them feel like they're okay, but in reality they aren't being fed properly — they're being starved to death and they don't even know it.

McChurch
And the church services were maddening. Every church was the same, like a fast food franchise. I'd go to church hungry for God's Word, but first I had to sit through a half hour of music. Who told them God wants to hear those boring songs?

Then the sermon. These days, it seems that everybody and his brother (and sister) wants to be a pastor. I'd say many of the pastors have *not* been called by God. Many of them are unlearned and lack understanding. And some are just buffoons; some are PhD buffoons. So with few exceptions, the sermons were unsatisfying. And once the sermon's finished, it's off to the coffee room to talk about the weather or baseball — anything but the Bible.

I'd leave church feeling like I'd just given blood. Instead of gaining, I felt like something had been taken from me. What if you went hungry to a restaurant and they only gave you a celery stalk? You wouldn't go back to that restaurant, would you?

I met so many people in churches who had been there for years, but who lacked a proper respect for the Bible, and whose understanding was muddled. I encountered men who didn't study the Bible but who, because of their personal magnetism, were put in positions of authority over baby Christians.

The Bible Quiz is born
As I studied the Bible I started thinking up questions that teach a lesson. I was also thinking about how I'd find people I could talk to about the Bible now that I found out that churches made me sick.

A couple of churches would go to the public square one night a week to give out food and clothing and give a short talk. I would run to them, so happy to be with fellow Christians, but I'd walk home feeling like I got stood up on a date. I started carrying a piece of paper with some of the questions I'd been coming up with. I made a little Bible quiz. I wanted to try it out on the people from the churches.

But I was not well received. One time someone asked me, "Where did you get that quiz?" He was very suspicious, as if to say, *Is that the authorized quiz?*

It was like, how dare you, a nobody, think you can interpret the Bible? How offensive. Circle the wagons. Get the women in the wagons. There's a stranger with an unauthorized Bible quiz!

It's the Word of God
One time, a member of a church said to me, "Oh, you're that guy who likes Bible trivia." See, that's the mindset these churches give people. That person wasn't taught the importance and the power of the Bible.
I corrected them. I said, "It's not trivia. It's the Word of God."

There was one person, though, who encouraged me. It's Stuart Diamond, who wrote the "Foreword from an observer" at the start of this book. He's a street preacher who's been on the street for decades, and who I'd known for nearly twenty years. Stuart loved my questions. Every time I'd see him, he kept saying, "Ask me a question." And he'd introduce me to people he knew and tell them about my questions, and I'd quiz them. I would write questions just for Stuart that I knew he'd enjoy. He's a unique Christian. In his street preaching and writings I can see that he has a profound understanding of who Jesus is.

God gives me
a street ministry

I felt I needed a lot of Bible study because my propensity to sin was so strong. I'd studied by myself for years, but now I needed to find others who love the Bible.

I had a new idea — go to Harvard Square and stand on a corner holding a sign that says:

Try My Bible Quiz?
Free!

That's how my street ministry began, in October of 2009. When I say "Free" — I mean that it's free in every way. I never asked anyone for money. I never asked anyone for anything. I was just there, standing silently, holding the sign.

My plan was to give people only as much Bible as they wanted, no more, no less. I never tried to give anyone something they didn't want. The question was — *would anyone stop and talk to me?*

Well, people did stop and talk, lots of them. And for the first time in my life I had something people wanted. Originally, I started doing the Bible Quiz for myself, because of the great pleasure I get from the Bible. But now I felt the great pleasure that comes from sharing truths from the Bible with others.

Giving people the Word of God
I made a decision about how I would do this. I know about the power in the Word of God. Hearing the words of the Bible is what changes people. I can't talk anybody into coming to Jesus. I can't give anyone a desire to study the Bible. So I would simply give people the Word of God, and what happens with it is between them and God. I just work here.

Being a street preacher has been a blessing to my Christian walk. I would tell people it's the best thing that could have happened to me. I would sometimes look at my display and think, *Where did that come from?* I felt like an observer. God did it. He directed my steps, made miracles. And I obeyed, I did my part. I would say to people, "I don't know why God chose me to man this post, but I'm so grateful He did."

When people ask me, "How long have you been a Christian?" I say, "Since before the creation of the world." There's never been a time in my life when I didn't believe in God. God has been on my mind from the time I was in my mother's womb.

Actually, I realized that the things I went through in my life made me into exactly the person God wanted for this assignment. God directed my steps, He knew me way before I was in my mother's womb. He knew me before He created this world. He set boundaries in my life, forced me to go in certain directions, made impossible things happen so He could move me where He wanted me to be (Romans 8:29).

I'm not talking about my sins. That's all on me, my fault. But God can even use that for good. That's a deep theological topic for another time. And no, I'm not saying we should sin so God can make good come from it. I would seriously advise against testing that theory.

On the street, I encountered so many different people, learned so much. You find out what's on the minds of the people. You're given reasons to dig into the Bible, to find the answers to hard questions. You get challenged, forced to answer people who accuse God of doing evil. I grew to love that challenge. What a blessing from God. You can't get that in a Bible school.

Moral support & encouragement
There was a certain man who was a regular in the Square. He would come and talk to me. He said he was glad I was there so he would have someone to talk to about the Bible. He had an amazing gift of

encouragement. He understood my ministry better than I did. He told me that what I was doing was better than being a pastor of a church.

And he's right. People in a congregation are pretty much all on the same page. But on the street you encounter all kinds, especially "hostiles" with no-holds-barred accusations and challenges, and you grow quickly. I was sharing the Bible with some who would never set foot in a church — people of various religions, atheists, skeptics, the mentally ill. That man's pep talks were just what I needed, and they would continue for the seven years that I did the Bible Quiz ministry in Harvard Square.

Homemade pamphlets

Passing the answers around

One day at the Quiz a man asked me if Jesus is God. Usually, when someone asked me a question, I would study at home and write something for them with Bible references to help them find the answer. So I did that for him. And then I thought, *I could make photocopies of what I write and display them in case anyone else has the same question.*

And that's how my pamphlets started. I would answer questions and expose false teachings. People have questions. They want to know what the Bible says, and they expect Christians to have answers. I wanted to give people what they expected a street preacher to have, which is why I also carried Bibles to give to people who asked for them.

Writing the pamphlets gave me a great new way to study the Bible. It brought me new paths into God's Word. It helped me become more familiar with the Bible and remember where certain passages are.

I would come to learn that when a Christian seriously starts to serve God, then God is going to give them just what they need to serve Him. And at just the right time. But I met very few fellow Christians who truly love the Bible. There was one, the best Christian I met in seven years, the exception. Karlos (his mom calls him Karly) has a childlike relish for the truths of the Bible. Karlos appreciated my providing a place on the street where Christians could meet, and hear and share the Word of God. He loved the Quiz questions and the pamphlets. We would talk Bible and dig into the Word. Karlos even gave me a name — Messenger of One. It means Messenger of the One True God.

Defender of the faith

The questions from skeptics, the accusations made by people against the Bible, turned out to be a great blessing for me. I became a defender of the faith. And I learned about the insidious cults that call themselves Christian in order to con people and draw them away from Christ. These cults put people into bondage to their man-made religions, their traditions. I learned that I needed to expose those cults, and warn people about them. Jesus did that, and so did the apostles.

My Christian walk was progressing by doing the street ministry. It gave me what I craved: I was getting fed the Word of God. I went home walking on air. It gave me so much to work with, to study, and to find answers to refute the lies people tell about God.

God opens new doors

But with all the good, I also had great disappointment. I met a lot of what I'd call Christian jokers — church people who came up to me as though I was some sort of curiosity. Groups of church people would walk by and ignore me, or stand at a distance staring at me with blank faces. They didn't understand what I was doing because they're not taught correctly in church, and the pastors don't impress upon them the importance of the Bible.

Churchgoers rebuke me

People I'd sat with in Bible studies would walk by me without even saying hello. Oh, they saw me. And church people became my biggest critics. Their complaint? I'm not a member of a church. They're just parrots who can't think for themselves. So they come and harass me when I'm trying to share God's Word with people. They've had it drilled into their heads that a Christian must become a member of a local church. Never mind the fact that in seven years well over ten thousand people either took my Quiz or took one of my pamphlets. It all counts for nothing, according to them, because I'm not a member of a church.

They would come and put down my street ministry. But what are *they* doing? Where are they? They're hiding within the four walls of their church watching *A Charlie Brown Christmas*. Oh, I'm sorry, they did come to Harvard Square to give out free hugs and granola bars. Going by my encounters with people from churches, I'm so grateful I did my own thing.

God gives me a wife

Church people became the bane of my existence. For two years I poured my time, energy, and money into the street ministry, and then I was burned out. I felt like I was flat on the mat, down for the count. And I blamed God.

I was fifty-eight and never married. I couldn't take one more day of loneliness. I wanted a wife. People would say, "You don't need a wife, you need God," and I'd say, "I *have* God — it's a wife I don't have."

And just like that, God gave me a wife, a Christian woman. I believe there's not another woman in the world who could do what my Vera is doing for me, for my ministry. And she's just the right editor for my writing. Now that I was finally serving God, He *finally* gave me a wife, gave me what I needed to serve Him, and gave me a companion.

So I continued doing the Quiz, but after seven years I looked at what I'd done and decided I could do better.

What next?
I had to spend a lot of time in Harvard Square dealing with people who wanted to debate biblical truths with me but who hadn't made the effort to understand those truths. Sadly, a lot of them were Christians. I met a lot of silly Christians who would argue with me by blurting out lines from the Bible out of context, lines they had no understanding of. This is what happens when the Bible is removed from society and when people are taught by bad pastors.

I wondered what came of my seven years of ministry. I'd gotten a great education out of it, but I wondered how much good it had done others. I'd written a lot of pamphlets by that time and covered lots of hard questions. Now I had a new idea. *What if my wife and I compiled the pamphlets into a book?*

A book with simple truths
With a book it would be possible to reach many more people. A book could go around the world, and reach those who are hungry for truth. I knew I had valuable things to say, and there are lots of people who would want to hear them. And that's the book you're holding, which contains biblical wisdom that I've acquired over the years, so far.

People who knew me in the past might say, "What? Bruce? He wrote a book about the Bible?" They might say, "But he did that to me," or, "He said this, and that. He's awful!" And, yes, I was awful. But God forgives me. Jesus came to save jerks. God is willing to forgive everyone. And God wants us to forgive each other.

The essence of Christianity

I'm clothed in the righteousness of Christ. I'm 100% righteous even though I sin every day, even though I mess up. I know, that will confuse some, and anger some, but it's the essence of Christianity, and if you come to understand it then you will be most fortunate.

Some will hate this book because they hate Jesus. Some will dismiss me because I lack a degree and church ordination, or because of my sinful past. Some who disagree with me will call me a heretic, a false teacher, even a hell-bound false teacher. Some will be enraged by this book, will call it fascism.

But this book is for you, the simple soul, the common person who loves the Lord and loves truth. When Jesus returns I'll be riding a white horse right behind Him. I want to see you riding the horse next to me (Revelation 19:14).

Newlyweds Bruce and Vera Benson

Study the Bible and think for yourself

Think for yourself? If you do, every denomination or culty church will scoff and accuse you of wrong thinking. But I'm not advocating wrong thinking. My intent is to free you from the restrictive homogeneous don't-rock-the-boat-by-thinking attitude found in almost every church.

Beware of any church that tells you you're not saved until they tell you you're saved. Beware of any church that says you can only study the Bible through them. The next thing you know, they'll be putting your hands in boiling water if they catch you reading the Bible on your own. Do not be afraid to study the Bible on your own.

Beware of any church or denomination that forbids or discourages independent Bible study, or forbids studying with a Bible translation other than their own.

Beware of anyone who tells you the common person can't understand the Bible. They'll say you shouldn't study the original Hebrew and Greek of the Bible — that it's over your head, that you're not worthy or capable, and it will only confuse you. In other words they imply: "Only we who went to Bible school and were taught what to think and how to think, are allowed to think."

Don't believe them. They are wrong. Christians have the Holy Spirit as our guide and teacher.

The church authorities did the same thing to Jesus. They said, "Why is He teaching the people? He never studied at our Bible school" (John 7:15). And they did the same thing to the apostles, saying, "Why are these unschooled amateurs teaching?" (Acts 4:13).

Here's the truth: Jesus is your teacher (John 13:13, 20:16; 1 John 2:27).

How to study the Bible

You cannot get a correct understanding of the truths in the Bible if all you do is read the Bible. You've also got to study the Bible. When I realized that, I prayed to God for help and He led me to books and teachers. If you're sincere then ask God for wisdom, and He will give it. God directed my steps. Ask Him to direct yours.

The first books that I bought to help me study the Bible were the *Strong's Concordance* and an *Unabridged Webster's Dictionary*. Then, over time, I added other books. I would always tell people there's no wrong way to study the Bible. I would read through the Bible starting at Genesis, and every time I read something that I didn't understand or wanted more understanding about, I would go to the books and read what they said about that passage.

I'm giving you a list of some of the books I've used. That doesn't mean I agree with everything they say. I don't. There is no Bible teacher that I agree with 100%. But I can still use their books. I can use the Bible references they give that relate to the passage I'm studying, their explanations, definitions of words in the original languages, and quotes they provide from other students of the Bible.

It's not that I'm thinking what they say must be correct because it's in a book. No, I'm just using these books to help me become more familiar with the Bible and to help me gain understanding. We have to do our hard work, studying, thinking, praying. And God rewards us by giving us the understanding. It takes two.

So, if you're sincere, then use my book to help you get familiar with the Bible. You don't need a seminary-trained pastor to tell you what God's Word says. God can tell you Himself. God's Holy Spirit teaches all Christians. A pastor is your servant, not your master. Christ is your Master. The pastor's job is to feed you the Word of God. But the pastor can't chew the food for you. You have to chew and meditate on the words, the truths of the Bible. You have to absorb the Bible yourself. Jesus is in that Bible, and *you've* got to have your relationship with Jesus. You don't have a relationship with Jesus through your pastor.

And how do you have that relationship with Jesus? You do that by doing the work yourself. Get your fingers into your Bible, dig into it, go back and forth through its pages. You have to get out your books and pen and paper. Search, seek, agonize, lie in bed sleepless. And that's how you get the blessings and strength. That's how you get fed. That's how you come to learn who Jesus is, what He expects from you, and how to do what He expects you to do.

God wrote the Bible, and He expects each person to read it, grow in understanding, act on it, and explain its truths to others.

> When I found Your words I ate them;
> and Your Word became my happiness
> and the thrill of my heart.   - Jeremiah 15:16

You might be thinking: *I don't know how to study, I've never studied, people tell me I'm stupid, I don't have an education from a school, I failed the IQ test.*

Well then, you're perfect. God will give you wisdom, and you will know things others don't. You'll know what matters and you'll learn how to apply that wisdom to everything in life. God's Word and His Holy Spirit will give you what you need to be able to talk to anyone. You will know the truth.

But, you say, the Bible's so big. Just start. Is knowing God important enough for you to take up a lifelong endeavor? Thank God if He lets you have His Word. That's a great gift. You'll be blessed (Amos 8:11).

I've benefited from the writings of fellow Christians, so this book is my contribution to encourage *you*. Finding others who are like-minded is comforting and uplifting.

Words of encouragement

My experience has been a long, amazing journey, my "Christian walk." God does the impossible in my life. He moves me from place to place, and He gives me what I need to serve Him, always at the perfect time. I'm so glad that God is doing it, because He does things far beyond anything I could imagine or could wish would happen. And it has all led to this book, which I'm certain is a work directed by God. I've given answers to a lot of the questions asked at the Quiz, but I couldn't have covered every question there is about the Bible. I'm writing a second book now which will be different from this one. It will focus on deception, and the ways the Enemy is leading people astray.

Pray to God and ask Him to give you the most precious gift, a love of the Bible. I hope you find your calling like I found mine. It's the best thing.

Persevere!

Don't be intimidated by someone because they have a PhD from a seminary. Don't assume they must be right and you must be wrong. You, a God-ordained person who has no church ordination, have just as much possibility of being right. PhDs can be wrong — and often are — and *you* could be right.

"What does it profit a man or a woman if they gain
a round of applause from society but lose their soul?"

- modern rephrasing of Jesus' question, Mark 8:36

God has not given us a cowardly spirit,
but a spirit of strength, love, and sound reasoning.

- 2 Timothy 1:7

Count the cost

In America, it's becoming more and more fashionable to portray Christians as evil people who should be shunned or punished. In parts of the world Christian men, women and children are being imprisoned, tortured, raped and slaughtered like animals.

We should pray for our fellow Christians constantly.

And we must be ever mindful of those who fight to give us the freedom to study our Bibles and practice our Christian faith. Many have given their lives.

Reference books that I use most

You can't repair your car if you don't have any tools. And you can't understand the Bible without tools. A superficial reading isn't enough. You need a concordance, lexicons, dictionaries, and commentaries. That way you can learn word meanings in the original languages, find cross references, and take advantage of the wisdom acquired by other students of the Bible.

BIBLES

The Companion Bible: *The Authorized Version of 1611 (KJV) with the Structures and Critical, Explanatory, and Suggestive Notes and with 198 Appendixes*, originally published 1922, notes and appendixes by E.W. Bullinger. Enlarged type edition by Kregel Publications. *The Companion Bible* is my favorite study Bible. E.W. Bullinger has packed this Bible with unique studies like no one else.

ESV Study Bible: *English Standard Version*, published by Crossway

The Apologetics Study Bible: *Understand Why You Believe. Real Questions. Straight Answers. Stronger Faith.* general editor Ted Cabal, published by Holman Bible Publishers

The Jewish Study Bible: *Jewish Publication Society Tanakh Translation*, edited by Adele Berlin and Marc Zvi Brettler

Teen Life Application Study Bible: *Go Where God Leads; New Living Translation*, published by Tyndale

The Evidence Bible *NKJV New King James Version: All You Need to Understand and Defend Your Faith*, commentary by Ray Comfort

1599 Geneva Bible: *Patriot's Edition,* Tolle Lege Press & White Hall Press

The Founders' Bible, *New American Standard Bible: The Origin of the Dream of Freedom,* signature historian David Barton, general editors Brad Cummings & Lance Wubbels. Contains in-depth explanations of the biblical origins of America's Christian roots.

The Interlinear Bible *including the Hebrew-Aramaic Old Testament and the Greek-English New Testament, With Strong's Concordance Numbers Above Each Word,* 4 volumes, general editor and translator J.P. Green

The advantage of *The Interlinear Bible* is that you can see an entire sentence all at once in the original language, with a literal English translation, word for word, written underneath it. You discover things such as when Jesus said, "It is finished" (John 19:30), in Greek it is just one word, *tetelestai,* "it has been finished." It gives you a deeper understanding than if you just read it in English.

CONCORDANCES

The main concordance used by students of the Bible is ***Strong's Exhaustive Concordance of the Bible*** by James Strong ISBN 0-917006-01-1.

There is also ***The Englishman's Concordance of the Old Testament,*** *Coded with Strong's Concordance Numbers* by George V. Wigram.

A concordance lists *every* Bible passage where *every* word in the Bible appears. For instance, you could look up the word "ark" in *Strong's Concordance.* You'd find that it appears in over a hundred places such as Genesis 6:14 where it refers to Noah's ark, and Exodus 2:3 where baby Moses was put into a basket which is also called an ark. Then when Moses was an adult, God told *him* to build an ark, the ark of the covenant, in Exodus 25:10.

After each biblical reference of the word you're looking up, *Strong's* provides a number so you can find it in the dictionaries at the back. An example: in 1 Samuel 28:6, the King James Version says Saul enquired of the LORD. Then 1 Chronicles 10:14 says Saul did *not* enquire of the LORD. It looks like a contradiction until you look up the different Hebrew words:

> And when Saul <u>enquired</u> (**#7592**)- of the LORD, the LORD
> answered him not.   - 1 Samuel 28:6 (KJV)

> So Saul died for his transgressions ... and also for asking
> counsel of one that had a familiar spirit, to <u>enquire</u> (**#1875**) of it;
> And <u>enquired</u> (**#1875**) <u>not</u> of the LORD.
>   - 1 Chronicles 10:13-14 (KJV)

Where it says that Saul enquired of the LORD, the word "enquired" is #7592. You look it up in the Hebrew Dictionary in the back and it's *sha'al*, to ask. Saul *asked* the LORD. Where it says that Saul did *not* enquire of the LORD, the word "enquire" is #1875 which is *darash*, to seek out. This is a stronger word than to ask, and implies a more fervent asking. When the LORD did not answer Saul, he decided to *seek out* the familiar spirit and *not seek out* the LORD. Saul's transgression was he *did not fervently seek out* the LORD, even though he asked Him.

There are other concordances based on the King James text which contain lexicons in the same volume, so I have listed them under lexicons.

LEXICONS

A lexicon is another tool to study the biblical languages of Hebrew and Greek. It's a type of dictionary which gives more than just the basic definition of a word and its derivation. A lexicon might also show how the word is used in a figure of speech, and give its grammatical case, voice, mood, tense, implications, and other valuable knowledge.

A Critical Lexicon and Concordance to the English and Greek New Testament by E.W. Bullinger

The New Englishman's Greek-English Concordance & Lexicon by G. Wigram and J. Green

The Brown-Driver-Briggs Hebrew and English Lexicon, Coded with *Strong's Concordance Numbers* by F. Brown, S. Driver, and C. Briggs

DICTIONARIES

The Complete Word Study Dictionary, New Testament, edited by Spiros Zodhiates

Smith's Bible Dictionary by William Smith. There are fourteen men in the Bible named Simon. The *Smith's Bible Dictionary* will tell you who each one of them were and where they appear in the Bible. This feature comes in handy when trying to distinguish the different kings of Israel who had the same names.

Theological Dictionary of the New Testament, edited by Gerhard Kittel. This ten volume work uses the numbers from *Strong's Concordance* and gives lengthy studies of New Testament words.

Fausset's Bible Dictionary by A.R. Fausset, co-author of Jamieson, Fausset and Brown's *Commentary on the Old and New Testaments*

American Dictionary of the English Language by Noah Webster, 1828 Facsimile First Edition, Foundation for American Christian Education. This is a Webster's Unabridged Dictionary from 1828, suitable for a Christian home and can be used by children. It does not have the obscene, sexually graphic language contained in the modern versions.

THESAURUS

The Synonym Finder by J. I. Rodale. I use this book constantly to find the right word.

SYMBOLISM

Dictionary of Biblical Imagery from InterVarsity Press, general editors L. Ryken, J. Wilhoit, and T. Longman

Figures of Speech Used in the Bible *Explained and Illustrated* by E.W. Bullinger. I love this book. It is an absolute must for any serious Bible student.

COMMENTARIES

A Commentary on the Old and New Testaments, 3 volumes, by Robert Jamieson, A.R. Fausset, and David Brown (known as *"JFB,"* *Jamieson, Faussett, Brown*). The *JFB* is a favorite commentary of mine. I love their old English way of saying things, the quotes from other scholars, and their amazing insights into biblical truths.

The MacArthur New Testament Commentary, 33 volumes, by John MacArthur. I use this commentary every day. It's an indispensable, vast resource for digging into the Word of God.

The IVP Bible Backround Commentary: Old Testament by John H. Walton, Victor H. Matthews & Mark W. Chavalas

The IVP Bible Background Commentary: New Testament by Craig Keener

Bengel's New Testament Commentary, 2 volumes, by John Albert Bengel

Why do I use the ancient King James Version?

Every Bible student must use the King James Version. Why? Because then you can use many resources to study the original languages. The King James Version (KJV) was *the* version, *the* Bible for centuries. So the scholars who wrote the word study books used the words of the KJV and the numbers from the *Strong's Concordance* that identify each word. This includes books such as *Zodhiates' Word Study Dictionary of the New Testament*, the *Brown-Driver-Briggs Hebrew Lexicon*, and others. I'm not saying I only use the KJV. But if I'm reading another version and come across a word I want to study, then most likely I won't find it in the word study books because the non-KJV versions use different words.

Online resources

My library of books has grown over the years. I must have at least 75 books that I use regularly to search out the truths of the Bible. I love my books, love using them, handling them. But I've also been blessed by Christian sites online such as the in-depth studies of www.preceptaustin.org.

The one I use the most is biblehub.com. You can study the original languages and read commentaries from scholars of the past. And of course online there's an unlimited amount of articles and commentaries on every subject you want to study.

An easy, inexpensive way to aquire books

The online store www.christianbook.com, Christian Book Distributors, is my favorite.

Index

G

H

Q

R

Acknowledgments

Thank you pastor Moses and Mrs Esther for your genuine Christian love

To my wife Vera, this book would not have happened without you
God put us together to make better use of the gifts He gave us

To the reader

I appreciate your interest in the Bible, and
I'm grateful you chose my book to help you.
Vera and I want *AHA moments from the Bible*
to change your life and ours.

I want to get something for myself out of writing
this book — to meet really smart fellow Christians
so I can ask them the hard questions I need
answers to.

Bruce Benson
bruce@harvardsquarebibleguy.com

98477506R00181

Made in the USA
Columbia, SC
30 June 2018